All About Motorcycles

(Abridged from
The Complete Motorcycle Book)

Deke Houlgate

Edited by George Engel and Marla Ray
Produced by Lyle Kenyon Engel

SCHOLASTIC BOOK SERVICES
New York Toronto London Auckland Sydney Tokyo

Photo Credits
"On Any Sunday," Bruce Brown Productions: pp. 47,
  98, 99
Escape Country Recreation Park: p. 170
Honda: pp. 159, 161
Yamaha: pp. 30, 44, 51, 54, 55, 57, 65, 70, 73, 83,
  104, 108, 111, 113, 115, 116, 119, 122, 129, 135

A hardcover edition of this book is published by Four Winds Press, a division of Scholastic, and is available through your local bookstore or directly from Four Winds Press, 50 West 44th Street, New York, N.Y. 10036.

1st printing . . . .   September 1975
Printed in the U.S.A.

Contents

Foreword

1. Taking It From the Top   1
2. I'll Have One of Each 32
3. Learning to Ride Is Easy 61
4. Survival Is No Laughing Matter 88
5. Simple Owner Maintenance 110
6. Safety, Ecology, Law,
   and the Cyclist 124
7. Two Wheels in Your Future 156

Foreword

Motorcycling is a pleasure, a thrill. It gives a person a great feeling when he knows he is able to master the power of an incredible machine. But it is not only for these reasons that the motorcycle has become an important part of American life.

The sport of motorcycling has come of age in the United States because the human being in a free society has a strong drive to assert himself. He wants to say, "I did it myself."

Riding a motorcycle is like flying an airplane. Motorcycles and airplanes are two of man's most demanding inventions. Learning to operate them gives a person the ultimate feeling of knowledge — to be able to control or master an awesome power. Becoming skillful later is all just a part of it. The baby delights in learning to walk, but he is even happier when he starts to run.

I have participated in many sports, but none of them gave me the personal satisfaction that motorcycling gives me. To make all of the swift, precise movements together that you must when operating a motorcycle, I believe, gives the rider unconsciously the feeling he is more capable than other persons who can't or won't ride a motorcycle.

That is why the phrase, "When motorcycling gets in your blood, you can't get it out," is true. Those of us who know it are proud of it.

This book by my friend Deke Houlgate, I hope, will encourage others who have never tried motorcycling to realize someday a little more of their own capabilities. May the greatest sport on wheels make their lives a little more complete!

Happy Landings,
Evel Knievel

World champion Roger DeCoster of Belgium shows good jumping form during a European motocross race.

A Swedish rider, left, two Russians (# 15 and # 16) and a West German muscle their way through an uphill curve at the Austrian world motocross championship event.

1. Taking It From the Top

Motorcycles and automobiles came into being for the same basic reason. Man, the tinkerer, wanted to perfect a self-propelled vehicle. Early automobile inventors started with wagon technology, which was fairly advanced, having undergone centuries of updating. The motorbike was based upon the more exciting, adventurous vehicle known as the velocipede, or bicycle.

It seems amazing that only one hundred years ago a far-seeing engineer was ridiculed or punished for talking loosely about the practical use of a self-propelled vehicle, but it did happen. There were a few inventive geniuses who built self-propelled wagons, bicycles and tricycles, but the products they made were largely experimental. Unfortunately for us, there was little written about those early attempts to make self-propelled cars and bikes, and only a few of the crude experiments survive today in museums and private collections.

It wasn't until the 1890's that the horseless carriage became sufficiently known by the public at large for a magazine to be published called *The Horseless Age*. The uncertain direction of the motor vehicle industry was revealed in the first issue of that periodical in 1895, as automobiles (four wheels) and motorcycles (two or three wheels) were poorly identified anywhere inside the covers. The self-propelled vehicles of the new generation were called, variously, *kerosene carriage, electric wagon, motor road wagon, petroleum carriage, vapor-driven horseless carriage, motor trap, business wagon, steam carriage,* or *ether bicycle.*

There were six three-wheel machines and five four-wheelers depicted in the issue that were called *motorcycles.* The word *automobile* did not come into general use until 1899.

Early "motorcycles" were mostly powered by steam, because the use of steam engines was more than one hundred years old at the time; but some of the early vehicles burned kerosene, and some were propelled through generation of hot air or electricity. One was set in motion by means of a coiled spring. All these self-propelled carts were crude compared to today's machines, but the great number of them and their variety of design left no doubt that the transportation revolution that was eventually to find man walking on the moon in the twentieth century was under way.

It would take a very wise student of history to decide which came first, the motorcycle or the automobile, partly because they were both developed at about the same time. The real reason we know so little about early automobile history and less about motorcycles of the same era is that the world at large paid little attention to either. We can only guess that three-wheeled motorcycles powered by steam were in somewhat general use in the 1830's in England. We think we know this because a drawing made in 1831 has been preserved that shows a park scene in which a number of steam-powered tricycles are puffing about. One expert on the subject speculates that artists of that day knew too little about engineering concepts to "invent" the steamcycle for their pictures, and that they must have had real models to copy.

Another historian guesses there were about one hundred steamcycles in use by 1830 in England, because both steam power and bicycle technology were well developed at that time.

Inventing a motorcycle in those very early days was a difficult task. First someone had to invent an engine that would work reliably. Then someone else had to come up with the idea that it could be used to propel a bicycle or a wagon. Still other inventive processes remained — for instance, how to modify the engine so it didn't have to be anchored to the ground near a tank of fuel or a reservoir of water, and how to apply the energy created by the machine to move the vehicle.

The earliest cycle known dates back to 1418. It was called a "manumotive" and was credited to Giovanni Fontana of Padua. It had four wheels and was operated by pulling an endless coil of rope connected to the rear wheels. Near the end of the seventeenth century, a Frenchman, Elie Richard, developed a carriage that called for the passenger to sit up front and steer while his servant operated a treadle in the rear which turned the wheels.

Meanwhile, in 1623, a brilliant Jesuit priest, astronomer, and missionary in charge of the Peking observatory, Ferdinand Verbiest, had become the first man to use the word "motor." He invented a steam turbine engine and described it this way: "This machine is a motor which makes it possible to bring into motion any apparatus to which it is attached."

Another early engineer suggested in 1690 that a self-propelled bicycle could be made to go with gunpowder. He was on to something, as rocket pioneer Robert Hutchings Goddard would prove little more than two hundred years later.

Another transportation pioneer wrote in 1784 of his idea to create a piston engine that would make use of air and turpentine that had been placed in contact with a hot surface so it would vaporize and ignite. More than one hundred years later, the most advanced motorcycles were still using this "hot tube ignition" principle.

Steam, however, was the first motive power to receive wide use on self-propelled cycles. William Murdock built his first three-

4

wheeler in 1781. Twenty years later Richard Trevithick built a three-wheel steamcycle he called "Puffing Devel," and took seven passengers for a ride on it.

Napoleon Bonaparte granted a patent on January 30, 1807, for a "fire engine," to Isaac de Rivaz. De Rivaz's internal combustion engine had already been perfected and in fact had once been destroyed by fire in 1788. A witness to the trial of the Frenchman's motor vehicle in 1804 gave this description: "(It) was not driven through the direct explosion of a gaseous substance, but by a motor that worked by means of those explosions in such a way that the vehicle moved forward in smooth motion and not by starts and jerks."

Not everything invented at the time was a step in the right direction. David Gordon of England invented something he called the "Squirrel Locomotive" engine in 1824. It had artificial horse legs to make it turn that worked like the legs of a squirrel running inside a cage. If that seems amusing, consider the advertisement for a three-wheel vehicle called the Cynophere, which appeared in magazines fifty years later in the United States. The Cynophere was powered by two dogs running inside the two rear wheels. This is how it was advertised:

Invented by M. Huret, of Paris, France, and Patented in the United States, December 14, 1875.

The Cynophere consist of two large wheels, between which is a comfortable seat and rest for the feet. In front is a small guide wheel, the direction being controlled at will by a rod held in the right hand, while at the left is a brake by which the speed is regulated. Power is furnished by a dog within each of the side wheels, and so light is the draft that it is no more exertion for the dogs to run upon the treadway of the wheel than it is to go at the same speed at their own pleasure. The French Society for the Prevention of Cruelty to Animals, to whom the subject was submitted by the inventor, unanimously endorsed the system.

The vehicle is light and graceful in its mechanism, and can be used by ladies and children, as well as gentlemen, without the slightest danger, discomfort or exertion. For pleasure purposes it is unsurpassed, and when fully introduced to the American public is destined to achieve a popularity far greater than that of the velocipede, while the moderate expense will bring it within the easy reach of all.

Imagine trading in the family six-cylinder sedan for a sporty Cynophere and a matched pair of greyhounds!

By the mid-1880's the idea of noisy, smoking, steam-hissing tricycles that frightened livestock and people alike was so offensive to most Britons that adventurous early riders often found themselves the targets of rock-throwers. Feelings grew so strong that soldiers occasionally had to intervene in disputes over steamcycles using the public roads. The result of emotionalism over the early steamcycles was curious indeed. The British people, who were at the forefront of the Industrial Revolution and enjoyed a tremendous technological lead over every other nation in the world, caused a series of laws to be passed that nearly brought development of self-propelled vehicles to a standstill for twenty years. In the late 1850's Parliament put into effect a 4-mile-an-hour national speed limit. The "Locomotives on Highways Act" required each motor vehicle to have three operators and a fourth man who was required to walk in front carrying a red flag to warn others on the road ahead. These laws were stricken from the books years later, but not before they became a laughingstock and were brazenly ignored. But in the meantime, significant motorcycle progress was made in Germany, France, and America, while the British saw their advantage slip away.

Joseph Etienne Lenoir was sixteen years old in 1858 when he built a 1½-horsepower gasoline-burning engine. He applied for a patent and received one on January 24, 1860. In 1863 he drove a four-wheel carriage from Paris to Joinville and back, a distance of 18 kilometers, in an hour and a half. The internal combustion engine developed rapidly after that.

In 1862 a Frenchman, Alphonse Beau de Rochas, published a paper describing the

Various views of action at a typical motorcycle recreation park, Indian Dunes Park, near Castaic, California. Racing and spectator areas are separated by permanent fencing, and some of the riding courses are used by both motorcycles and dune buggies. Also separated are riding trails and competition tracks, to enhance safety.

operation of the modern four-stroke engine. A working model of the four-stroke was patented in 1876 by Dr. N. A. Otto of Germany. Dr. Otto's development was to have a profound effect on both the motorcycle and automotive industries, because of the influence it had on one of his assistants. He was Gottfried Jellinek, a brash, rebellious young man from a well-to-do family. He soon quit Otto's employ to found the Daimler-Benz Company in Germany, first as a manufacturer of motorized bicycles and later as one of the world's great auto making companies whose products bear the proud tri-star of Mercedes-Benz today.

Meanwhile, the steam-powered bicycle became a reality in America about 1869, when Sylvester H. Roper of Roxbury, Massachusetts, built what he called a velocipede. Fortunately, the three-wheel machine has been preserved by the Smithsonian Institution in Washington, D.C., and can still be seen today. Primitive though it was, it worked. The steam was heated over a vertical fire tube that hung in the center of three wood spoke wheels. Steam rushed out to push a set of two piston rods, which were connected to 2½-inch cranks on either side of the rear axle. The front wheel, connected to the rear wheels by a wrought iron fork, had a straight handlebar with wooden grips. The operator was supposed to reach down and insert lumps of coal into the fire box through a small round door at the side.

Roper was another whose life was threatened when he took the steamcycle out on the roads near his home. Neighbors had him arrested for frightening their horses, but he was always released by police when he pointed out that there was no law on the books forbidding the operation of his machine. Townspeople lobbied with the city council and got an ordinance passed, but it was quickly repealed when the council was reminded it had appropriated $5,000 for the development of a steam-powered fire engine.

Sylvester Roper continued building steamcycles through 1896, when he was seventy-two years old. His last model developed a fantastic (for that time) 8 horsepower, and carried him at speeds up to 40 mph. So proud was he of his motorbike that Roper entered a local bicycle race and left the others behind in a trail of soot and smoke the first lap around the one-mile track. As he began the second lap, the steamcycle wavered and crashed. Officials reported later that he had apparently died of a heart attack.

Just before Roper built his first steamcycle in 1869, a Frenchman named Michel was credited with developing a velocipede powered by steam called the "Bone Shaker." It had a one-cylinder engine driving the rear wheel. J. H. Knight of Farnham, England, built a steam tricycle in 1874, but he didn't get around to making another one for twenty years. Sir Thomas Parkyns built a steam tricycle in 1881, exhibited it at a London cycle

11

show, and received several orders from prospective buyers. Another Englishman named Meek built a steam three-wheeler in 1887.

In Philadelphia, the enterprising Lucius Copeland began adding steam engines to bicycles and selling them. He had invented a steam engine with a condenser on it in 1884. The condenser converted steam back to water and thus stretched the range of the motorcycle. It was quite a revolutionary idea for its day, since almost all steam engines were "open" and merely dissipated steam into the air. This required that they stop frequently to fill up with water. The condenser gave Copeland a silent one-half horsepower motor that emitted no smoke or visible steam while scooting him along at 12 mph. He went to Arizona, California, and finally New York before finding backers for his steamcycle. He opened a plant under the name of Northrup Manufacturing Company and produced two hundred bikes.

Count Albert De Dion, a distinguished sportsman and pioneer of both the motorcycle and automobile industries, built his first steam tricycle in 1884. Seven years earlier, the famous champion of steam cars, France's Leon Serpollet, had built a three-wheel steamer, but it wasn't until 1889 that he made history when he drove a friend from Paris to Lyon in it. In 1879 George A. Long of Northfield, Massachusetts, built a steam engine, which he mated the next year with a frame and running gear to be the prototype of the

Columbia steam bicycle made for the Weed Sewing Machine Company of Hartford, Connecticut. His patent for a "steam road vehicle" was granted on July 10, 1883. Long's contraption was a reverse tricycle with the single driving wheel in the rear and two spindly wheels up front. It took two people to operate it safely. The Long Steam Tricycle on display at the Smithsonian is believed to be his original effort.

The first gasoline-driven motorcycle was either the work of Gottlieb Daimler in Germany, Edward Butler in England, or De Dion in France. Of the three, Daimler is generally considered to be the father of the modern motorcycle for the invention of his incredibly crude and unwieldy two-wheeler.

As we pointed out before, inventing the engine solved only one-fourth of the problem. A motor for a self-propelled vehicle had to be small and light. It needed an economic fuel supply that could be carried with it. And it needed some mechanism to connect it with the wheels on the ground. Most internal combustion motors of the day were connected to a stationary fuel supply and could not be used. Sparking had been tried, but storage batteries necessary to provide electricity were too large and heavy to be practical on a motorcycle. So Daimler had to devise a method for igniting the gasoline inside the combustion chamber of his single-cylinder engine.

What he decided to do after "endless tests and unremitting pursuit of the objective," as he put it, was to pass the gasoline vapor over a hot metal surface while forcing air into the chamber. To do this Daimler inserted a thin tube into the cylinder, and at the bottom of the tube, outside the cylinder, he lighted a Bunsen burner. The flame turned the tube red hot, and the heat was transferred into the chamber by conductivity. It was quite an ingenious scheme, but its reliability and safety left something to be desired. Today it might be described as giving the engine a "hot foot" to make it go.

The Daimler motorcycle also had outside support wheels, which could be likened to the training wheels of today's bicycles except that they could be raised at will, and a tiller for a steering mechanism which was not all that different from the handlebars found on later motorcycles, bicycles, and tricycles.

The first person to test Daimler's two-wheel machine was his son, Paul, who rode it 3 kilometers from the factory in Cannstatt to Unterturkheim. The trip was uneventful, but a short time later Daimler's nephew, Otto Zels, stole the motorcycle for a joy ride and had a hair-raising experience.

Young Zels had watched his cousin light the Bunsen burner and studied how to crank the engine over with the right side of the crankshaft. He pulled back on the control handle, which engaged the clutch and tightened the belt drive. All that he had seen before, and so he knew the operation up to that point. What he didn't know was how to apply the brake, and it didn't occur to Otto that he didn't possess this vital bit of information until he came to a downhill run and began picking up speed.

At the bottom of the hill was a wide curve leading into a narrow street. He steered the motorcycle over to a fence and, like the Grand National stock car driver does today, tried to lean into the wall and scrub away speed. Alas, all he did was scrape his arm. Ahead of him, to his horror, was a horse-drawn cab virtually blocking the entrance to the narrow street. The cab driver had seen him coming, had panicked and stopped right where he could not be avoided. At the last minute the cabby came to and realized he should try to move out of the way, but it was too late.

On impact Zels was thrown headlong over the horse, but fortunately he was unhurt, flipping completely over and landing on his feet. To keep the cab driver quiet, for he was guilty of riding the motorcycle without the owner's permission or knowledge, Zels paid for damages and gave the cabby a sizable tip. In an awkward sense, he had just made history. Zels had survived the first known traffic collision on a motorcycle and paid the first recorded out-of-court settlement. He was also the first man in history ever known to steal a motorcycle.

Motorcycles of the Englishman, Butler, and De Dion in France were built about the same time. De Dion was said to have completed his first three-wheel lightweight in 1884, and Butler to have invented and patented the gasoline-burning tricycle the same year. However, it took Butler until 1887 to build his cycle, which had two wheels in front.

In 1892, J. D. Roots of England built the first tricycle powered by a two-stroke one-cycle engine, a motor which was invented in 1881 by Sir Dugald Clark. It was ingeniously cooled by water which flowed to the engine through the tubes of the frame. By 1894, Darracq, the famous early French auto manufacturer, began producing and selling the Millet motorcycle. The first four-cylinder motorcycle was produced in 1896 by Colonel H. C. Holden of Great Britain.

One of the most interesting early motorcycles was invented by Louis S. Clarke of Pittsburgh, founder of the Pittsburgh Motor Vehicle Company, later to be known as the Autocar Company. In 1897 he built an experimental three-wheel carriage to gain the experience he believed he needed to produce automobiles. His gasoline engine drove the two rear wheels. There was no throttle. He controlled the speed by use of a spark arrester. The fuel tank was located under the saddle, where it is found in most models today.

In the years immediately preceding the twentieth century, the motorcycle industry had its share of get-rich-quick speculators, as did the auto industry. Many of the pioneers were quick-thinking promoters who had the vision to take chances at the brink of new technology, to jump in where more conservative businessmen dared not set foot. At the same time, there were those conniving money hustlers who were just as anxious to ride the motorized bandwagon by preying on the gullible and excited public.

In 1896 an American promoter, E. J. Pennington, arrived in England to make and sell his motorcycles. One of his early prototypes got airborne during a test, and it gave him an idea that would make his product the most talked about motor vehicle in England during the months to come. He commissioned an illustrator to draw a poster which showed the Pennington Motor Bicycle sailing over a river, frightening a number of observers, including two men in a rowboat directly under the cycle. The inspiration for this drawing, which appeared in an extravagant advertising campaign, was said to be the accidental discovery that a motorcycle can actually fly for some distance through the air. Pennington himself claimed it had flown a distance of 65 feet. This, it may be noted, occurred some six years before the Wright brothers actually did fly at Kitty Hawk, North Carolina.

Pennington bikes operated at a minimum speed of 8 mph, a top speed of 30, and were regularly demonstrated at the Coventry bicycle track. Before he could get the motorcycle into production, Pennington sold his patents to another speculator, Harry John Lawson, for 100,000 pounds sterling. Shortly afterward, however, the press, which had faithfully recorded all the wild claims of the inventor, became disenchanted with Pennington. An expose of his operation ruined him, and all of his companies collapsed.

The 1890's was a decade of rapid engineering progress. The motorcycle, automobile, and bicycle industries all benefited from the 1888 invention of the pneumatic tire by John Boyd Dunlop. The inflated tire was in general use by 1895, a year when the De Dion engine replaced its "hot tube" ignition system with electrical works. Widely copied by other engine designers, the one-half-horsepower single-cylinder De Dion engine was the standard of the industry. By 1894, the German firm of Hildebrand and Wolfmuller were also commercially producing a gasoline-powered motorcycle in Munich. In 1896, Great Britain's Parliament passed the so-called Emancipation Act, which removed the last of the unreasonable restrictions against motor vehicles and raised the national speed limit to 12 mph. A historic motorcycle race held in England soon afterward was named in honor of the Emancipation Act.

Harry Lawson, the entrepreneur who had paid so much for patent rights to the Pennington motorcycle, had anticipated repeal of his country's ridiculous anti-motor vehicle laws and had begun to purchase patents, licenses, and rights to every seemingly worthwhile invention he could get his hands on. One of his acquisitions was the De Dion engine, which he made for various motorcycles he produced under the banner of British Motor Syndicate. Lawson's companies made and sold the Accles, Beeston (King George V helped to popularize motorcycles by riding one on January 28, 1898, while he was still the Duke of York), Humbers, and Bollee. Lawson had created a sort of British General Motors, and he produced not only motorcycles but automobiles (that came out of factories known as the Great Horseless Carriage Company), and Daimlers. He also produced the first auto show in 1896. Ironically, all of these companies went out of business in a very few years, but Lawson is remembered today as the founder of the motor vehicle industry in England.

If any predictions can be made about a motorized vehicle, it is that man will find a way to race it and a way to make war with it. The first motorcycle race of international significance was that Emancipation Run in England in 1896. By 1899 The Simms "Motor Scout" was in action in the South African Boer War. The Simms had four wheels, carried a Maxim gun and 1,000 rounds of ammunition. It had a fuel range of 120 miles and was used by dispatch riders.

Beginning in 1897 many motorcycle engines were "clip-ons," which could be affixed to a bicycle, either in front or in back of the rider. The motors rode high, were inconvenient, made for an uncomfortable ride, and adversely affected either the weight distribution or the center of gravity or both. The best clip-on engines were made by Menerva of Belgium and Werner of France. Werner clip-ons were found on such early British motor-cycles as the Enfield, Quadrant, and Triumph. In 1901 the Russian-born Werner brothers built in France the first engine that was an integral part of the bike. Off dropped the bicycle pedals, and the motorcycle began to take on that distinctive appearance it retains today. The Werner, of course, was widely copied.

The Werner featured a spray carburetor. Lubrication was accomplished by means of a hand pump. Riders of Werner-powered cycles learned the tricky art of judging when to pump the oil. On a flat surface they would pump every few miles, more often if the cycle were climbing a hill and had to work harder. Some very astute riders learned to figure when the oil needed pumping by the amount of blue haze in the exhaust smoke or by the feel of the engine. They could feel the engine tighten just before it was about to seize due to oil starvation. Another innovation of the Werner was the foot pedal that operated the rear brake, and the brake, which was nothing more than a block of fiber that pressed against the rim of the wheel. This type of brake was common for the first twenty years of this century. Slides were common on the Werner, because there was no neutral, and when the wheel locked up, the engine stalled.

American motorcycle history, except for

those early artifacts mentioned already in this chapter, really began in 1900 with the meeting between bicycle manufacturer George Hendee and mechanic Oscar Hedstrom.

Hedstrom worked on one of the pacer motorcycles that were used by bicycle racers in Madison Square Garden and other bike tracks of the day. A pacer was a motorcycle with a broad plank on the back that was used to cut wind resistance and create a vacuum so the bike rider could travel fast more easily. In fact, bike riders were actually drafting on the motorcycles, having learned the secrets of aerodynamics in racing through their sense of feel—the pressure of wind against their bodies.

Because of the nature of their work, pacer motorcycles had to last for long distances. They needed to be trouble-free. Sitting in Madison Square Garden one night watching the races, the thought occurred to Hendee that a man who could build a reliable pacer might be the ideal person to develop a reliable motorcycle that could be sold to the public. After a race in December, 1900, the two men met, and Hendee asked Hedstrom if he thought he could build such a machine. Hedstrom, of course, said yes. They wrote a contract agreement on the back of an old envelope Hendee had been carrying in his pocket, and both men signed it. The American motorcycle industry was born.

Hedstrom went to his home in Middletown,

Connecticut, and began design work on the first successful American machine. The following spring his prototype was built and ready for testing. Hedstrom had already tested the bike near his home, but the final trial was to take place at the bicycle factory in Springfield, Massachusetts. A large crowd of curious spectators lined Cross Street hill, which had a 19 percent grade. Hedstrom started at slow speed and accelerated up the hill without a hitch. He deliberately slowed down at the steepest place on the hill, practically stalling the engine, then opened the throttle to demonstrate the reserve power his machine possessed.

A delighted George Hendee immediately leased loft space and began to manufacture the motorcycle, which carried one of the most distinguished names the industry has ever known. The Hendee motorcycle was called the Indian, in honor of the noble Red Man who was the true pioneer of America.

Considering the modern trend toward lightweight bikes with high compression engines, the 1901 Indian was years ahead of its time. Weighing only 98 pounds, it had a 1¾-horsepower engine that gave it good acceleration, instant response, and a wide speed range. Only three machines were made that year, but production really got under way in 1902, when 143 Indians came off the assembly line.

Hedstrom, who had been a bicycle racer before he began building pacer motorcycles, urged that the Hendee Manufacturing Company plunge into racing to advertise its product. On May 30, 1902, Indian won the Ft. George hillclimb in Bronx, New York, and on July 1-3 of that year George Hendee, Oscar Hedstrom, and a Springfield dealer, George Holden, finished first-second-third in the 250-mile New York-to-Boston run, the first marathon race ever held in this country.

About the time the first Indian prototype was being assembled in Oscar Hedstrom's garage, two friends got together with an idea in Milwaukee, Wisconsin. Their idea was to take the hard work out of bicycling. Bill Harley worked as a draftsman by day, and Arthur Davidson was a pattern maker. On their own time, with the aid of a German draftsman who knew about European motorcycles and had a working understanding of the De Dion engine, they tinkered.

Soon they acquired more help. Art's brother, Walter Davidson, was persuaded to join the project. Walter was a skilled mechanic working as a railroad machinist in Parsons, Kansas. Then came William, a toolmaker, and they had to move their operations to a small shop owned by a friend. Another volunteer who contributed his ideas to the building of that first Harley-Davidson motorcycle was Ole Evinrude, who later became famous in the small craft industry as the originator of the outboard motor bearing his name.

The original Harley-Davidson had a 3-horsepower engine, very powerful for its day, but the partners found that when they tried to climb a steep hill they still had to help it along with their feet. They had started the project with the idea of taking the hard work out of bicycling, so they decided the motor needed to be more powerful, and they went back to work increasing the piston displacement to get more horsepower output.

Harley and the Davidson boys found they were once again running out of room. William C. Davidson, the boys' father, was a cabinetmaker. He built a 10- by 15-foot building in his back yard so they could continue work. The boys hung a sign over the door when it was finished: "Harley-Davidson Motor Company."

The first three Harley-Davidson motorcycles were sold before they were assembled in 1903. A man named Miller bought the first one completed. He rode it for 6000 miles and sold it to a George Lyon, who rode it another 15,000 miles before selling it to a Dr. Webster. He added 19,000 miles, sold it to Louis Fluke who rode it 12,000 miles. The machine was last known to be owned by a Stephen Sparrow who put 32,000 miles on it.

The small company grew slowly, increasing production to five motorcycles in 1904 and to eight in 1905. The shed in the Davidsons' back yard had grown to four times its size, but it was overrun with cycle parts. A factory site had to be found.

Securing property on the site of the present factory, the boys framed up a building 28 by

80 feet alongside a railroad spur. Rail employees thought it was too close to the tracks, went to the trouble of surveying the area, and proved they were right. So the Davidsons got together a gang of eight or ten husky young fellows, picked up the framework of the shop, and moved it back a foot and a half.

Like all growing young firms, Harley-Davidson needed capital. In the early 1900's it wasn't too easy to walk into your neighborhood bank and say, "Hi there. I'm making a great new product called a motorcycle, and I'm interested in a loan." But the company did survive that difficult period quite easily. The resourceful Davidson boys went to an uncle in Madison, Wisconsin, who they knew had enough capital, and borrowed it from him. Because he was a beekeeper, they called him their "honey uncle."

In the final analysis, the success of any manufacturing company depends upon the quality of its products. At the time, Indian and Harley-Davidson were only two companies in an industry that became quite crowded early in this century. One of those early companies was Reading-Standard, which boasted in its advertising: "Manufactured and tested in the mountains." One wiseacre added, "Tested in the mountains, all right. It must have been tested downhill."

Other early competitors were Orient, Wagner, Rambler, Dyke, Tribune, Steffey, Yale, Auto-Bi, Columbia, Shaw, Curtiss (the aircraft company founded by aviation pioneer Glenn Curtiss), Duck, Pope, Mitchell, Greer, Holley, Minneapolis, Marathon Marsh, Merkel, and Miami. A company which made one of the classic motorcycles was Excelsior, founded in 1911. It lasted twenty-one years but fell victim to the Great Depression.

Motorcycle companies here and abroad prospered in the years between 1900 and the start of World War I, when many of their important engineering advances were made. Motorcycles truly improved from year to year, but their prospects for survival during the greatest transportation revolution the world has ever known were poor indeed. Motorcycles were sold in those early years as basic transportation, and as such they could not compete against the automobile.

During this exciting period, 1900-1915, rawhide and leather drive belts were replaced by chains, the magneto was adopted, the sprung front fork and kick starter were invented, a three-speed gearbox was tried, and so was a variable speed transmission. The 1914 Indian Twin used an electrical system which ran the lights as well as the ignition system, eliminating the bothersome gas lamp.

Accelerating the engineering advances of the period and the popularity of motorcycle racing everywhere was the advent of the Isle of Man Tourist Trophy, the world's most important motorcycle race. But as suddenly as the motorcycle boom began in the burst of engineering creativity at the start of the century, it died with the start of World War I. Twenty-five makes of American motorcycles disappeared from the scene between 1915 and 1917.

World War I marked the first time in history when broad use of motorcycles was made by military forces. Triumph produced 30,000 motorbikes for the British army, and the American Expeditionary Force had 10,000 motorcycles, mostly Indians. NSU made a lightweight machine for the Kaiser's army. It's interesting to note that armies have made less and less use of motorcycles since then. The U.S. Army had an inventory of about 5000 bikes at the start of World War II. This figure had dropped to about 1000 by the mid-1950's, when they were used almost exclusively for traffic control. In Vietnam during 1969, a reconnaissance unit of the 25th Infantry actually introduced motorcycles to combat as an experiment! Officers were surprised to find the recon riders could cover three times as much ground in a day as a foot soldier, and they were pleased to discover motorcycles were very effective on the narrow bicycle trails used by Viet Cong supply personnel. The VC, on the other hand, also knew the value of motorcycles in their terrorist activities. The throwing of grenades and bombs from motorcycles became such a problem in Saigon that authorities made it mandatory for a motorcycle passenger to ride sidesaddle. That way, they reasoned, it would be more difficult to hide a bomb, and the passenger would find it more difficult to balance himself. Thus, he would be hampered from throwing a deadly missile or firing a weapon.

In World War II during the Normandy invasion, the British battleship H.M.S. *Rodney* stood offshore lobbing in shells at the direction of a spotter plane. After knocking out all the important targets, the pilot continued to direct only one of the ship's nine 16-inch guns. Each time the battleship fired, the pilot would radio back, "Up a thousand." After several rounds, each one fired 1000 yards farther inland, the ship's gunnery officer became curious and inquired what was the target at which he was firing.

"A dirty Hun, sir," came the reply. "He's on a motorbike, and he's heading inland as fast as his two wheels can take him."

It remained for the post-World War II era to produce a revival of interest in the motorcycle, not as a specialized mode of transportation, but rather as a recreation vehicle. Leadership in this development came from one of the world's most unlikely places, Japan.

Japan had been a backward, feudal country which refused to join the outside world and resisted any attempt of others to establish contact until America's Commodore Perry sailed into Tokyo harbor with his gunboats in 1854. The successful Japanese race to catch up with other industrialized nations of the world since that time is well known, but its early ventures into motorcycling were so insignificant that the rest of the world ignored them.

The first motorcycle, a steamer of unknown origin, was imported into Japan in 1899. Narazo Shimazu designed and built the first Japanese motorcycle engine in 1908, and the first company to make a complete motorbike was Miyata in 1913, but Miyata suspended production of its two-wheeler in 1916. A handful of companies were building only 3037 a year in 1940, and in the devastation of war they could assemble only 211 in 1945.

Into this vacuum came a school dropout mechanic who had raced automobiles until a serious accident forced him to quit. In 1947 at the age of forty-one, Soichiro Honda contemplated his hard luck. He had been a successful piston manufacturer, but the Americans had destroyed his factory by bombing. Rather than heap self-pity on himself, he began to look around for a product he could make which would have a market among his countrymen. He hit upon the idea of manufacturing a motorbike, which he started to do by buying five hundred war surplus generators and attaching them to bicycles. Pretty soon he had sold all five hundred and there were no more generators to buy. So he designed his own motorcycle.

Honda launched his business in two board shacks in a bomb-shattered district of Hammamatsu with thirty-four employees and $2777 in the bank. Weathering one financial crisis after another (Japan has business recessions, too), Honda built a business that has meant a worldwide boom to the motorcycle industry and has been the backbone of Japan's postwar export expansion.

Today's motorcycle bears quite a resemblance to its early antecedents. A fellow who travels in Europe every summer visited a museum in England, where several examples of early motorbikes are on exhibit along with the later, more exotic products of the country's well-respected motorcycle technology.

"You know," he said, "I couldn't help thinking that despite all this talk about styling, one motorcycle looked pretty much like every other one."

The basic design of motorcycles hasn't changed much in half a century, as can be seen from this view of a 1919 Cleveland.

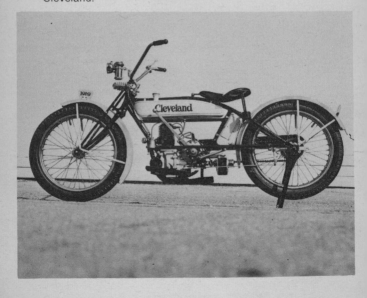

It's true they all have two wheels, a motor, a seat, and handlebars, and it's also true that motorcycles today are vastly different from the two-wheelers of an earlier generation. However, the biggest difference is that motorcycles in today's society have changed their function. No longer must they be depended upon for basic transportaation. They are go-anywhere machines that invite the rider to the open road, the countryside, the mountains, the desert.

Today's motorcyclist has a limitless choice of destinations. He can enjoy an infinite variety of riding experiences. For some motorcycle manufacturers, it took half a century to discover what any enthusiast could have told them in a minute—the motorcycle is more than a method of transportation; it's also a fun machine.

2. I'll Have One of Each

A used-car salesman of our acquaintance once told us there are only three kinds of automobile buyers: One wants to own a particular make of car, one wants to pay a certain amount for his car, and the other wants to pay so much a month. The first fellow will walk onto the lot looking for a Ford. He might drive out in a Model A or an LTD; it doesn't matter what year, what it costs, or how much mileage is on the odometer. The second buyer has $800 to spend, and he wants an $800 automobile, no matter if it is a foreign sports car, a station wagon, a two-door sedan, or a pickup truck. The third fellow, even more poorly advised than the other two, wants to make payments of $65 a month, and he'll buy anything the salesman offers him so long as he can get it on those terms.

Too often the novice motorcycle buyer approaches a showroom without even as much of an idea about what he wants as our three used-car shoppers. The most common mistake of a first-time buyer is to walk in and ask the price of the biggest, most expensive ma-

chine in the place. If good motorcycle salesmen were like the car guys, they'd have this
fellow's gold fillings out of his mouth in ten
minutes.

The big, fast bike has the glamour, the
mystique. Possibly it is the machine he first
read about in one of the motorcycle magazines which consistently play up the hot performers. In any motorcycle dealership the
most publicized machine on display is usually the Ferrari of the line. Fortunately for our
unsuspecting buyer, the good dealer or his
salesman will ask a few discreet questions
about his riding experience and usually try to
talk the real amateur down to a smaller, less
potentially dangerous machine.

The slightly more sophisticated buyer
makes another mistake, going for a machine
that isn't adequate to his needs. The reason
he does this, according to one top-notch
dealer, is that he doesn't think about the
"long range usability" of his motorcycle.

"He buys what a friend told him he ought to
have or what a salesman sold him on," the
dealer said. "He doesn't look ahead a year
and a half or two years to see what he is going
to do with the bike or whether or not he is
going to enjoy it. Most first-time buyers and
even many second-time buyers really don't
know what they want when they come in the
door."

Price sometimes plays a factor in this
buyer's choice of machines. He knows that
too small a bike isn't legal to ride on the

freeway or expressway. So he gets a machine that just barely meets the minimum and then, the dealer said, "goes out and runs it on the freeway and shortens the life of the machine."

Just like the three "marks" of the used-car salesman, the average motorcycle buyer is either swayed by the sex appeal of a big brute machine, is hooked on price, or takes bad advice. He forgets to think for himself about why he is buying a motorcycle and what he wants to do with it after he gets it.

One of the first mistakes the first-time purchaser makes when talking with the salesman is not admitting that he doesn't know how to ride. This is an understandable ego hang-up, because it is embarrassing to many people to have to admit they don't know how to do something. The salesman, however, knows right away if he is dealing with an intelligent customer when he hears him speak those difficult words: "I've never ridden one before."

Sammy Tanner, the well-known racer, once sold motorcycles for a dealership in Long Beach, California. One day a man in his forties drove up in a Cadillac with his good-looking girlfriend and began browsing.

After some hesitation the fellow did state he had never ridden a motorcycle before. Noting he was nervous talking about it in front of his pretty female companion, Sammy suggested they retire to a side street so he could get some instruction. The man showed good aptitude and learned quickly the rudiments of handling the motorcycle. After a while his tension vanished, and Sammy thought he was ready to buy. That's when the customer rode the bike back onto the lot where his girlfriend was waiting and apparently decided to show off.

Opening the throttle, he roared down the narrow space between the bikes on display. Suddenly he froze at the controls and couldn't stop, crashing into a row of new machinery, bouncing up onto a display stand, and destroying the bike sitting on it. The terrified customer spotted the driveway and tried to aim for it but missed and hit the side of the building next door. The noise brought everybody in the shop out to the lot to aid the victim, who lay somewhat groggy and bleeding on the sidewalk.

"Let's get you to the hospital," Sammy said. "Oh no, I can't go to the hospital," the man insisted. No matter how many argued with him that he should have medical treatment or at least an examination, he stood his ground. He wouldn't go. Finally Sammy asked him why.

"I haven't got the time," the customer said. "I'm on my way down to the unemployment office to collect my check."

Sammy Tanner learned later that the expensive car his "customer" had driven to the agency that day was stolen.

Most salesmen, who are after all working for a commission and are responsible for sales rather than the safety record of the motorcycle riders of the world, are very good about making sure a customer can handle the equipment he is buying. However, the minute a buyer says he knows how to ride, the salesman will back off and not question him further, because he is interested in making the sale and doesn't want to do anything to discourage it. That's important to remember.

A good salesman, once having made the sale, will give the customer a thorough checkout on controls and the functions of important components of the motorcycle. He will talk about simple maintenance and usually supply the buyer with either the owner's manual or a simple brochure that tells about care and maintenance. At that time he may learn that the customer doesn't know how to ride, and usually will take time out to give a quick course in basic riding. He's not paid to do that. He is sincerely interested in making sure the customer is happy, because a happy customer is a repeat customer. But theoretically every minute the salesman spends away from the showroom floor is time he could be spending making another sale.

It's also a sad but true statement that fully 50 percent of all motorcycle buyers do not ask for a briefing on the controls. In those cases, it's the well-trained, thoughtful salesman who volunteers the information and refuses to leave the customer alone until he is convinced that the buyer knows what he is doing on the motorcycle.

Despite the good intentions, however, somewhere in the United States today there is probably a new motorcycle owner riding off the dealer's lot, blipping the throttle and sailing into the back of a parked car.

We mentioned earlier "long range usability." One of the most common errors a buyer makes is not knowing what he is going to do with the motorcycle when he buys it. It might help to know just what is available, to know something about sizes, weights, different horsepower, and torque characteristics of the available machinery. We'll try to discuss each type of motorcycle a little later in this chapter.

But first let's examine the price-shopper. There is certainly nothing wrong with touring from one dealership to another to see which offers the best "deal." The average price of a new motorcycle works out to about $600, which usually buys a motorcycle in the 125 to 175cc range. That's a lot of money to commit to anything, particularly for the young man of sixteen to twenty-five who makes up the bulk of the motorcycle market.

The motorcycle retail business is much like the automobile business in this regard. Auto dealers long ago gave up trying to make buyers pay the so-called "list" price. In fact, they have encouraged price chiseling to the extent that manufacturer's suggested prices are almost a fiction today. Shrewd shopping for a motorcycle will likely produce a savings, because motorcycle dealers, like their auto agency cousins, shave prices. A dealer might also reduce or eliminate preparation and destination charges, or offer attractive terms to win the buyer away from his competitors.

Shopping is an accepted practice, but one thing to keep in mind is that after the purchase comes service. A new motorcycle owner would be smart to buy where he expects that service to be performed.

Human nature being what it is, a dealer hates to have a bike purchaser shop his store, go out and buy from another dealer, and then come in and expect warranty work and other service privileges. If at all possible, buy from a dealer who has a good service operation. Most warranties are standard contracts calling for a period of ninety days or so when all parts and labor for product failure are to be provided at no cost to the purchaser. Warranties usually extend to one year or 5000 miles, whichever occurs first, and they cover serious failures but not routine servicing. Since warranty work is something that is spelled out not only in the contract between the buyer and the dealer but also between the dealer and the factory distributor, they can be relied on to give the customer what he has coming regardless of what the dealer would like to do. It's a lot more pleasant, however, to have the man caring for your motorcycle sincerely thinking of your best interests.

So how does a buyer select a "good service" dealer, one who will give him courteous treatment, charge him fair prices, do reliable work, and sell him quality replacement parts and accessories?

One quick way to tell is to step back into the service department and take a look. Dealerships vary in size from "mom and pop" stores to large establishments employing nearly one hundred people. If the service department has more than a handful of employees, if there is a lot of work in progress with some backlog, and if it is neatly laid out and just looks efficient, chances are it's a good service dealership.

On the other hand, if the place is dirty, if only one or two mechanics are on duty, if there is horseplay or obvious malingering going on, if the layout is cramped or sloppy, if tools and testing equipment are not stored neatly, or if there is little backlog of work on the premises, the customer might be hesitant to trust his new machine to this dealer.

The final test, before actually taking a motorcycle in and having it serviced or repaired, is to talk to someone who has had work done there. There is no way for a motorcycle dealer to keep all his customers happy, but it is impossible for him to keep unhappy customers from talking about bad experiences they've had. If someone you know was not satisfied with the dealer in question, he'll surely talk about it.

An important factor in the selection of a motorcycle that is frequently overlooked by the buyer — but hardly ever by the good salesman — is size.

A good rule of thumb for the first-time owner is that he is better off with a machine that is close to his own weight and has a comfortable wheelbase. The fellow who is 5 feet 4 inches tall and weighs 140 pounds would have a difficult time wrestling with anything heavier than 250 pounds. On the other hand, a 6-foot 2-inch 225-pounder needs the long wheelbase of a larger machine to keep from cramping his legs, and he certainly should be big enough to handle the extra weight of a big bike.

It is a bit much to expect women, who generally weigh between 100 and 125 pounds, to be comfortable handling anything over 150 pounds.

In the process of analyzing what kind of motorcycle to buy, the beginner could do worse than talk with experienced motorcycle riders. They've made the mistakes already, and like all enthusiasts and hobbyists they are happy to talk about their equipment and the riding enjoyment they get. Motorcyclists are not hard to find. There may be one in the neighborhood. They are found in school and office parking lots. They are likely to go to motorcycle races, go camping in resort areas, and attend club events in nearly every community. A list of clubs, their addresses, and their events are often found on the newsstands in weekly publications like *Cycle News* and *Motorcycle Weekly*.

What the beginning rider should learn quickly is that there are two basic kinds of motorcycles, those for the street and those for off-the-road riding. Although some machines are adaptable to both, most models fall into one category or the other. There are several types of street machines, off-road bikes, and so-called street scramblers. Let's take a look at some of them:

Motorcycles for the Street

These are primarily designed for enjoyment on the open road, but the latest models are on their good behavior in low speed, stop-and-go conditions found in crowded cities as well. Street bikes are likely to have two cylinders instead of one, come equipped with a longer seat so two people can ride, carry larger fuel tanks, and have tires with a normal tread design. Exhaust pipes travel from the motor underneath the feet and straight back. Engines of most models are designed so that the motorcycle can hum along at the speed limit effortlessly with lots of power to spare.

Manufacturers offer a number of comfort-oriented accessories, such as fairings to break the wind, buddy seats, handgrips, back rests, windshields, and even radios. They also offer such cross-country touring gear as saddlebags and luggage racks.

All street bikes are not large, heavy honkers, but come in engine power choices down to the minimum horsepower required for use on freeways and expressways (some with even fewer horses) and to a total weight of less than 150 pounds.

There is a noticeable difference between a street bike (left) and an off-road motorcycle. Note the smooth tire tread on the street version, compared with the knobbytype tire at right. Although motorcycle tires are round, not flat, street treads are more like automobile tire treads. A long street saddle gives comfort to two riders, while an off-road motorcycle typically carries only one person. The easiest detail to spot is the placement of the exhaust pipe. It is low and below the rider's feet on a street machine and high on the off-road bike to avoid rocks and water.

The American manufacturer Harley-Davidson is generally associated with bulky 500-pound machines that require a muscular giant to push up the street, but Harley offers handsome 65, 125, and 350cc models that weigh from 140 to 259 pounds. Japanese manufacturers have a variety of street machinery that runs the entire range of engine size from 50 to 750cc (4½ to 67 horsepower), and several British makes are world-famous for the high quality of their road bikes. Except for Bridgestone, which makes street bikes as small as 100cc of piston displacement (11 horsepower), the Anglo tradition runs to larger, long-range touring bikes.

A confirmed honker enthusiast might argue the point, but if the beginning rider intends doing much traveling in heavy traffic, he might be better off shopping for one of the lighter, less powerful machines. Coming to a legal stop and putting the foot down is a lot easier when the bike weighs 250 to 300 pounds than when it hefts a solid 700 pounds of steel, plastic, and rubber. The smaller the engine, however, the slower the cruising speed, and the less comfortable a rider is likely to feel in the fast lane.

Motorcycles for Off-the-Road

The off-road bike has a different job to perform, and therefore it is engineered quite differently. The gearing is close ratio, and the power curve extends upward to the highest engine speeds, but it is notable for good low end torque that gives quick acceleration at low speeds. This is needed in a rough and tumble environment for which it is built.

It's easy to tell an off-road machine from a street bike by looking at the tires. Dirt bike tires have knobs one-half inch square in place of the street tread. The exhaust pipe is also a dead giveaway. It slants upward from the header and passes under the fuel tank and seat.

Look closer at the off-road machine, and other factors show up. The frame is light — the largest desert racing machines weigh in under 250 pounds — and there is also invariably only a one-cylinder engine. The suspension is sprung more loosely. The front fork has a five-inch travel or more, and the rear shocks have two to four inches of give. Engine sizes, and thus horsepower potential, run the gamut from 50 to 500cc depending on the specialized use for which the machine is built. And there are several uses.

Sportsmen have created a demand for a go-anywhere bike that can be used to reach remote hunting and fishing sites. This type of conveyance is also rugged and powerful enough to haul back such game as deer, elk, and bear. So-called trail bikes are good for climbing, although they are not designed for speed, even on the flat. They are useful for herding livestock, and the U.S. Forest Service has been experimenting with their use on fire trails for years. Another breed of motorcycle enthusiast prefers the trail bike, the trail ex-

A hunter demonstrates typical off-road use of a trail bike. Note the bird which is slung from the handle bar.

plorer. In this group are people who don't particularly enjoy dashing about like a jackrabbit over rocks and gullies but merely like to ride up trails to see what is at the other end. Many geologists and nature lovers are in this group. They find pleasure putt-putting about in the wilderness, taking in the sights, or collecting specimens.

The street scrambler is used about nine-tenths of the time on the street, but is adaptable to the dirt. It is heavier than the usual off-road machine and is therefore a little more difficult to handle over rough terrain. A scrambler owner can easily learn to change wheels and make rear shock adjustments to improve the handling when switching from the asphalt surface to dirt or back again.

A special kind of non-racing competition, trials riding, has developed a completely different breed of off-road bike, the trials machine. The object of trials is to cover a terribly difficult obstacle course without removing the feet from the footpegs. Each touchdown is called a "dab" and is counted against the rider. The toughest trials include water hazards as well as a diabolically conceived series of dirt, sand, mud, and rock obstructions. The favorite trick of the people who lay out trials courses is to find a fallen log that is three feet or more in diameter and guide the course over the seemingly impossible obstacle. Good trials riders clear such logs with ease. The trials machine has a small fuel tank and very small footpegs, which are miniaturized to prevent their striking the ground. The trials engine is built for strong low end torque but with no necessity for a high top speed, since trials riding is done mostly between 10 and 20 mph.

The Racing Bike

A friend of ours refused to buy his teenage son a motorcycle to ride back and forth to school because he said it was too dangerous, but he did get him a racing bike.

"I don't worry about him on the race track," the man said. "The riders are all excellent, they are going in the same direction, and there are no 4000-pound automobiles to run into."

This isn't a recommendation to start the youngster out on a racing bike, but it might be a good thing to know something about competition machinery. Racers come in all sizes, from 50cc to 1000. There are even mini-bike races with no age limit. Racing is as diversified as pleasure riding, and a variety of frames, suspension systems, gearing, and engines are available for most makes of motorcycles which produce racing models.

The classic machine is the road racer, which started out in development half a century ago as a street machine and evolved from there. Engines are exotic and tuned to the most precise settings possible. Handlebars are the small clip-on type. They feature huge brakes, either drum or disc, and they have larger than normal fuel tanks, usually about five gallons. The frame is very light, the steering is lightning fast, and the rider crouches behind a streamlined fairing that often has been designed in a wind tunnel for maximum aerodynamic efficiency.

On the dirt ovals are found the Class C flat track bikes, which are light but extremely rugged motorcycles with specified engine sizes that are designed to turn primarily in one direction, to the left. Normally they have four-stroke engines and weigh about 200 pounds. In 1971 the rule forbidding use of brakes was rescinded, and by the end of the season about half of the touring pros had disc brakes on the rear wheel. Flat track bikes also feature a quick-change rear axle to allow for rapid sprocket and wheel swaps to adjust to local track conditions. A specialized type of

Dragster bikes, like this Harley-Davidson twin, cover the quarter-mile in less than 9 seconds and hit speeds over 170 mph while the rider wiggles back and forth, partly to achieve balance and partly to apply more weight to the rear wheel for better traction. Note that the frame is specially built and is much longer than a stock motorcycle frame.

dirt track racer is the Class A speedway bike, which has a superlight rigid frame weighing less than the motorcycle engine and a fuel-burning 500cc motor that is only good for sprints of less than two miles of racing at one time.

The TT (Tourist Trophy) motorcycle is designed specifically to turn left and right on a dirt course that meanders in tight curls and has a jump to negotiate. There are strong disc brakes front and rear, and the engine is built with lots of low end torque and horsepower.

As for the ultimate dirt racing bike, it is the motocross racer. It is tough, reliable, extremely well balanced, and light. It is likely to have a 21-inch front wheel in place of the stock 19-inch front wheel and huge brakes front and rear. Motocross bikes are also very light, weighing 230 pounds or less.

Slightly different, but built much the same, is the desert racing machine, which campaigns in such events as the Mint 400 and the Baja 1000. Because it travels longer without stopping, it has a larger fuel capacity than a motocross bike, and because it is designed to run at 70 to 80 mph over incredibly rough terrain and to handle well in the loose dirt and sand, it has a 19-inch wheel.

One more type of competition machine remains, the drag bike, which is designed for one purpose only, to cover the quarter-mile in the shortest possible time. It is usually home-made to the lightest possible specification, including replacement of steel with such exotic metals as titanium, vanadium, and aluminum. Usually all-out drag bikes have two or three engines, either mounted one behind the other or side by side. The rear tire has a flat surface like an automobile tire. The handlebars are clip-ons, and the seat is usually a sheet of aluminum the rider lies across, wiggling his weight back and forth, partly to stay upright and partly to force more weight to the rear wheel to improve the traction. A half-gallon tank carries either gasoline or nitromethane, depending on what class the motorcycle is competing in.

What About Engine Sizes?

By automobile standards motorcycles have tiny engines, but they also make possible fantastic power-to-weight ratios by comparison. This power-to-weight superiority is what makes motorcycles such exciting performers.

Let's compare the American pony car's V8 horsepower of 250 with its 3000 pounds of weight to a street 250cc (16-cubic-inch) motorcycle putting out 25 horsepower and weighing 220 pounds. The car has about a 1 to 12 power-to-weight ratio, while the ratio for the motorcycle is about 1 to 9. That's a dramatic difference.

Piston displacement in motorcycles and automobiles can be compared in the same way a thimble might be set up alongside a water glass. The size differences are so great that it is impractical to translate motorcycle piston displacement into the cubic inches listed for American automobiles. Nearly all motorcycle engines are measured in cubic centimeters, from the smallest 50cc motorbikes and minicycles to the 1200cc kings of the road. To make a comparison, simply remember that 1 cubic inch is equal to 16.387 cubic centimeters. To put it another way, 1000cc or 1 liter is equal to 61.025 cubic inches. It would take the displacement of twenty Harley 250s to equal that of one Mustang 305-cubic-inch V8.

It is generally, but often incorrectly, thought that the more inexperienced the rider, the smaller the engine he should have at his disposal. On the contrary, the 50cc engine with a slow throttle response takes a great deal of skill to master, since a motorcycle becomes more and more stable as it increases speed. Manipulating a small bike requires good concentration and coordination to keep it constantly in the most efficient driving gear. On the other hand, a beginning rider is courting trouble if he climbs on a big engine monster and roars down the highway.

Like most good things in life, moderation in the selection of a motorcycle engine is the best course to follow. The middle range is hard to beat, 125 to 250cc.

The Helmet and Other Accessories

A new motorcycle may cost anywhere from $400 to $2500, but every smart rider knows the next $20 to $50 he spends is the most important cash outlay he will make. This is the cost of a reliable safety helmet. Some states require the use of helmets, but it shouldn't matter if they do or not. The helmet covers the most vital area of the body, the part we think, see, talk, hear, eat, and smell with, and the part that is the most vulnerable to severe and even fatal injury.

We use the term "reliable" rather than

An essential in motorcycle safety is a helmet. A large percentage of motorcycle accidents result in head injuries when helmets are not worn, and head injuries can be serious and sometimes fatal. Rider (top, left) displays a typical helmet and also wears protective glasses. Rider (top, right) also wears a helmet but carries with him dark goggles for day wear and clear goggles for night riding. A woman rider (left) puts on a different type of helmet, which covers less of her neck and face.

"approved," because there is some current controversy over so-called "approved" helmets. Every safety helmet sold in a motorcycle shop meets a voluntary standard set by the American National Standard Institute known as Z90. The controversy exists over policing, as there are claims that some manufacturers do not maintain the high Z90 standard after having attained it and passed the initial test. The industry itself has moved to correct this oversight by forming a group called the Safety Helmet Council Association that plans to enforce the proper labeling of Z90 approved helmets.

Meanwhile, such a distinguished journalist as Ivan Wagar, editor of *Cycle World*, has reported that Z90 approved helmets have been taken out of shipping crates fresh from the factory with cracks in them or have been damaged merely by falling off the showroom shelf. That's hardly good enough performance to make you want to entrust a human skull to one of those brain buckets. The SNELL 1970 standard is more rigorous than Z90. Several companies, including Bell & H.A., make helmets which meet this standard.

The most reliable material used in the manufacture of a helmet is fiberglass, and it might be wise to stick to it until the controversy has been resolved. The questionable material at this point is an injection molded polycarbonate, which under normal conditions would be hard as a rock, and would probably exceed fiberglass for toughness.

However, polycarbonate is susceptible to cracking when exposed to solvents, gasoline, and a number of other substances, and it requires some caution in handling, cleaning, and storing to prevent damage.

Helmets are available in a number of designs. Some helmets cover only the cranium, ending at a line just above ear level. Most of them cover the ears and the neck. The best is said to offer full face protection. It has a strip which joins the left and right sides of the headpiece just below the nose, effectively covering the mouth and chin.

Just as vital as head protection is eye protection. It is up to the rider to decide which of two types of eye coverings he prefers and then to use one of them every time he rides. Goggles, which can cost less than a dollar to as much as $10, are the usual means of covering the eyes. They should be made of plastic rather than glass, to prevent splintering on impact of some foreign object, which inevitably implants small glass fragments in the eye.

Most helmets are offered with a button-on option, the plastic face shield. These are particularly recommended to a rider who must wear prescription glasses. Face shields are available in clear or tinted plastic, giving the rider the option of wearing a tinted shield to cut down glare during the daytime or a clear shield for night riding.

Gloves are recommended for the same reason eye protection is strongly suggested. A large bug, a stone, or other object may fly at a motorcyclist at any time, and a surprise stinging blow could easily cause the rider to take his hand off the handlebars at precisely the wrong moment, causing a serious accident.

It should hardly be necessary to advise a motorcyclist against going barefoot or wearing tennis shoes, but it is surprising how many riders risk broken feet, sprained ankles, and worse by ignoring the simple reality that the ground is harder than the human foot, and it is frequently pockmarked with holes to snap an unsuspecting toe. Footwear should be leather, and lace-up boots are strongly recommended for off-road use, as well as being required for racing. Why lace-up boots? Try taking off a pull-over boot over a swollen, sprained ankle sometime.

Shoes are important in motorcycling, as shown here (left) where a well-protected foot, encased in a strong boot, is caught by a rock. Light footwear like tennis shoes (right) offers almost no protection and is not recommended.

Adjusting the rearview mirror, a very important safety device and one that is difficult to use properly on a motorcycle.

For street riding a must option is the rearview mirror. It is difficult to use effectively on a motorcycle, but it is not only required for street licensing, its use on a motorcycle is even more protection than the rearview mirror in an automobile. The rearview mirror hopefully prevents that awful moment when the rider must turn his head backward to see what is happening behind him. That's a harrowing experience at best.

An accessory that has become a stock component for any motorcycle licensed for the street is the turn signal. It became mandatory for all street bikes beginning with the 1972 model year.

Most other accessories are either "dress-up" items, kits for modifying the bike for specific use, or comfort add-ons. Any dealer carries a full inventory of these products along with his supply of spare parts for repair or maintenance. For the do-it-yourself motorcycle owner, there are also speed shops and even motorcycle parts discount houses in nearly every major metropolitan area.

A Word About Minibikes

What a great toy for a youngster! Right? It's small and doesn't travel very fast, so it must be safe. It's maneuverable enough to be operated in the driveway or even the front yard. Well, it's fun, all right, but a minibike can be one of the most dangerous toys a young boy can get from his doting parents.

It's one of the most ill-handling motorbikes there are. The average minibike has a wheelbase that is too short, wheels that are too small, and a poor center of balance. Most minibikes are also top-heavy, giving them a natural tendency to want to crash. Even experienced riders have taken headers off them.

Some minibikes have a braking system that consists of a metal plate that rubs against the rear tire, which of course is made of rubber. Frames are often boxy and not intended for standing up to severe jolts. The standard power plant is a lawnmower motor, which was never intended to be used in a minibike and consequently is subject to breakdown because of this harder use.

The manufacturers got together to define minibikes so that they could be differentiated from another popular class of recreation motorbike, the minicycle. They decided that a minibike generally has a tire height of 14 inches or less, solid disc hubs, a seat height of about 25 inches, and a motor limited to about 4 horsepower. Some minibikes are very well constructed, but nearly all of them suffer from those handling deficiencies built into a short wheelbase, small wheel, top-heavy design.

At the same time, the manufacturers defined the somewhat safer and more reliable minicycle as a vehicle with a tire height of 18 to 23 inches, a two- or four-stroke motorcycle-type engine, spoked wheels that have standard motorcycle-type front and rear brakes, and a three-speed or slipped clutch transmission. Of course, there are smaller bikes that have one or more of the minicycle features.

Most motorcycle dealers also sell and license motorcycle trailers like this one.

As might be expected a minicycle costs substantially more than a minibike, but purchasers have often found that they have a safer product, less subject to failure, and possibly costing the same or less in the long run than a minibike.

Buying a Used Motorcycle

A good used motorcycle depreciates 10 to 20 percent the first year, but may not lose any value after that, which is a lot better than an automobile does. Still, there are good bargains to be found if the buyer is willing to take the time to search for what he wants, and if he is knowledgeable enough about mechanical things to know what problems to look for in a used motorcycle.

Our friend Bob Greene, editor of *Motorcycle Sport Quarterly*, once listed some handy guidelines to follow when checking out a piece of used machinery. Here is Greene's twelve-point recommendation on how to find serious trouble before buying it:

1 *Look for bearing failure, which shows up in the oil.* Take an oil sample out of the crankcase and pour it into a white porcelain pan and gently shake it around in the pan like a '49er looking for gold. If there are metal particles in the oil, they will settle to the bottom, and you know that motor will soon be history.

2 When firing up the motor, listen for strange noises. If they are not readily apparent, take a screwdriver and use it as a stethoscope, placing the tip against the motor and putting your ear up to the handle.

3 Pull on the drive chain. If it can be taken off the rear sprocket, it's had it.

4 Look for fork bearing wear. Placing a block under the motorcycle, have someone sit on the saddle and shift his weight back and forth. Face the front wheel and grab the fork legs. Try to move them back and forth. They shouldn't move, unless the bike has had many miles or has been abused.

5 Elevate the rear wheel and let it run free. First, take each side of the tire and twist it back and forth. If there is real movement, there is wear in the swing arm pivot bearings. While you're in position, also spin the rear wheel and eyeball it, checking for a bent rim.

6 Check frame alignment by sighting from the front wheel to the back with head down on the ground in front of the motorcycle.

7 Look for brake wear by checking the angle of the brake arm. If it has a 90-degree angle or not much more, most of the adjustment is gone.

8 *Look undernearth the motorcycle for those invisible underside dents and flat spots.* They may not be important, but added to a lot of other problems they may.

9 *While underneath, look for telltale signs that the motorcycle has been repainted recently.* Sometimes that means it was painted to cover up crash damage. A new paint job could be an asset rather than a cover-up, and it must be evaluated.

10 *Check the head cone bearing, which is between the top fork bracket and the frame.* While holding the brake on, rock back and forth. Touching the bearing with a finger, feel for any movement.

11 *Unbolt the zerk fitting and look at the grease.* If it is dry, chances are the bike was abused by its owner.

12 *Look at the battery case.* If there is a dirt build-up from the floor of the case to where it touches the bottom of the plates, the battery is probably not long for this world. Non-transparent cases can be judged by the condition of the fluid in the battery. Look out for muddy fluid. That's bad news.

So there we have it — how to buy a new or used motorcycle. It just takes common sense, a little advance planning, honesty, and some healthy skepticism.

3. Learning to Ride Is Easy

The trouble with learning to ride a motorcycle is that most of us have to teach ourselves. Until recently there wasn't any organized movement like high school driver education for the novice motorcyclist. Today, fortunately, there are more than 2000 high schools in the United States offering some sort of motorcycle rider education. In the state of Minnesota, attendance at a rider training school is mandatory. The U.S. Navy has recently adopted a program, and there are a number of universities which have a similar course of instruction.

All this is a drop in the bucket, however, when the number of students is compared to the number of new riders who enter the sport of motorcycling every year. Under the circumstances, it is amazing that the accident record hasn't multiplied itself out of sight. Claims of the National Safety Council to the contrary, motorcyclists have an excellent safety record, a record that has been achieved in the face of fantastic growth in the number of riders. Growth of motorcycling means only one thing — every new rider is somebody who hasn't ridden before. And the statistics tend to prove that new people are more likely to have serious accidents.

The reason rider education, or lack of it, seems to us to be neglected is based on our own experience. An importer lent us a 175cc bike for a weekend several years ago and, when we went to pick it up, asked almost as an afterthought:

"By the way, have you ever ridden a motorcycle before?"

We had to confess, no.

"You won't have any trouble," the man said. "It's very simple."

Then he proceeded to give us the short course on the operation of a motorbike that was capable of speeds in excess of 70 mph. First he explained the controls, then asked us to ride in first gear around the parking lot next to his warehouse. He watched us make three perfect circles, and he congratulated us. He explained the operation of the gearshift and asked us if we wanted to try riding it around the block. Of course we did.

So off we went, riding this beautiful machine which had yet to record 10 miles on the odometer through one of the most heavily traveled industrial neighborhoods of Los Angeles during the afternoon rush hour. Not having had cause to think about the implications of what we were doing, we blithely rolled out into the maelstrom of tanker-trucks, homeward-bound passenger cars, buses, and pickups. Meanwhile, we tried to practice smooth up- and down-shifting and master the tricky feel of braking. Within five minutes we were smoothly moving along with the traffic at 50 mph.

When we returned to the warehouse, our smiling benefactor waved at us and said, "I think you've got it all right. Go on and ride it home. Remember, take it easy and you'll be all right."

Now the pressure was on. We suddenly realized that a couple of decades sitting behind the steering wheel of a wide variety of automobiles didn't mean anything anymore. We were going to have to travel from Point A to Point B, a distance of about 15 miles, on a motorcycle we barely knew how to ride. It meant concentrating on gears, throttle, brakes, traffic lights, other vehicles on the road, speed limits, pedestrians, small animals, wind resistance, changes in road surface from one block to the next, litter in the streets, potholes, side street traffic, and all the rest. Meanwhile, we had to keep the brain racing to try to figure out the shortest, safest, least likely to be patrolled streets (we didn't want to attract a traffic ticket either) between the warehouse and home sweet home. That was the most careful and at the same time most exciting 15 miles we had ever covered.

Reflecting on the experience later, we guessed that this was equivalent to what many new motorcycle riders go through when they take their first ride. We wondered how many bad accidents are caused by sheer ignorance. Later, when we learned enough about motorcycles to realize what we had done while mingling with some of the most aggressive motor vehicle traffic in the world, the thought was frightening.

There are various gradations of motorcycle rider training. Most good dealerships train their salesmen to look for amateurs and give them rider familiarization courses whenever practical. The trouble is many "first time" customers have done just enough riding on borrowed bikes that they can't benefit from that minimum amount of instruction. One manufacturer, Yamaha, has organized familiarization riding into a regular school curriculum, with twelve hours of classes, mostly riding, spread over four consecutive Saturdays. Riders completing the course are also required to read a very good basic book, *Common Sense Tips for Safe Sportcycling*, by Jimmy Jingu and Don Gately. When they finish both, they are capable of passing any licensing test required in the United States. Many of the schools which have begun training programs, as well as the U.S. Navy, have adopted the Yamaha training format.

There is a school in Toronto that has far more stringent standards. Before graduation students must be able to handle obstacles, such as tire casings thrown in their way, and they are required to balance themselves on a teeter-totter while riding a motorcycle over it. The school emphasizes survival in a hostile environment, and in many ways that is what motorcycling is all about.

In 1968 a branch of the Los Angeles City School System, the West Valley Occupational Training Center in Woodland Hills, California, became the first known public school enterprise to start a course in motorcycle riding. It is still in operation, the instruction consisting of six Saturday sessions for a total of twenty-four hours divided fifty-fifty between the classroom and the outdoor "laboratory." Cooperating with the center are the Motorcycle Industry Safety Council, the state's Motor Vehicle Department, the Automobile Club of Southern California, the Los Angeles Police Department, and San Fernando Valley State College. If it weren't for the outside assistance, there would be no public school system involvement since the center is supposed

A woman runs through the operation of the motorcycle while it is still up on its kickstand, so that she will be thoroughly familiar with the controls when she begins to ride.

to train men and women for employment. Graduates are advertised to the business community as safe, reliable messengers, but it is unlikely many of the students in motorcycle riding are taking the classes to prepare for a career as delivery boys.

All of these schools plus any others we don't know about couldn't handle more than 30,000 riders a year. In the state of California alone, from 1964 to 1969, motorcycle registrations increased 128 percent, from 208,362 to 476,919. And that doesn't even count off-road bikes that don't have to be registered!

So most of the new motorcycle riders are just going to have to do the best they can, seeking help from motorcycle salesmen, experienced riders, their local police traffic divisions, and by reading various publications available on the subject.

Perhaps the first thing to learn about a motorcycle is that you shouldn't be in a big hurry to jump on it and ride it. Knowing the natural enthusiasm a person has for a new possession, that's easier to preach than to practice. We'll never forget that wonderful Christmas so many years ago when Santa Claus brought the first two-wheel bicycle to our house. We pushed it out to the sidewalk, finally taught ourselves how to flip a leg over it while it was rolling, and started pedaling down the pavement. We were actually riding a two-wheeler! There was only one thing wrong — we neglected to learn what made it stop.

So when we got to the end of the block we

did the only thing we could improvise on the spot. We aimed the bicycle for a bush and jumped off. After a few rides up and down the block, we got rather good at jumping off and crashing the bike on target — into a shrub. It was almost a letdown to learn that we were doing it wrong, that there was a brake to push on.

Fortunately, most beginning motorcycle riders do not practice this sort of foolishness, but there are many examples of their making mistakes because of unfamiliarity with the machine, its controls, its handling character-istics, and its safe operation. It is one thing to listen to a fellow say, "This is the brake, use it this way," and fully another to do it when you have to.

Instead of hopping on a motorcycle and learning the hard way, walk around it and look at it first, then climb on it, get the feel, and try the controls.

The most important control is down at the right side on most motorcycles, below the footpeg. It is the foot-controlled brake for the rear wheel. The reason the rear brake is the most important one for a beginner to know is that operation of the front brake is a little tricky and needs getting used to. You should know enough about the front brake to stay away from it at first, if nothing else. It is operated by squeezing the lever on the out-side of the right handle-bar toward the hand-le bar.

Leaving the bike on its kickstand, hop on

and sit in the saddle. Reach out and grip the handlebars while resting the feet on the foot-pegs. The right handlegrip is twisted to open and close the throttle. Outside the left handlegrip is the lever controlling the clutch. The foot opposite the brake manipulates the gear-shift, which is usually three to five speeds forward. Not all gearshifts operate the same way. For specifics, consult the owner's manual. Most motorcycles have a kick starter on the right side, although some now carry an electrical starter.

Just as an automobile has an ignition key, so do most motorcycles. To start the bike after turning the key on, it is necessary to make sure the petcock found on the bottom of the fuel tank is turned to "on" so gasoline can get to the carburetor. Also make sure the transmission is in neutral. Some motorcycles have a green light on the face of the speedometer which turns on to indicate neutral. Otherwise, it's easy to tell by gently rocking back and forth to see if the rear wheel is free or locked. If it is free, you're in neutral.

If the motor is cold, be sure the choke is out all the way. Otherwise, it's a good thing to engage the choke at least part way when starting the bike. The choke should remain open only thirty to forty-five seconds, and the engine should be run a little above idle for two or three minutes until it warms up, sometimes longer for one of the bigger bikes. If the choke is opened too soon, the motor will probably die. If it is left closed too long, you'll soon know it, because the spark plug will foul.

All kick starters behave differently, and some work differently every time. For best results, crack the throttle about one-quarter of the way, then push down hard with the right foot. Leave the foot on the starter peg, because if it kicks back that will prevent a painful cut or bruise on the leg. The motor should start at least after the third kick. If it doesn't start, forget the whole thing. Something is wrong. Most smaller bikes, those up to 350cc, will be easy to start, and the kick starter is not likely to kick back. But if you're a conservative, you'll leave that foot planted on the starter peg to prevent kickbacks, just in case.

During the familiarization process, it is a good plan to have someone with you who knows about motorcycles, so you can ask questions, and so he can observe errors you make before it is time to try riding the motorcycle. When that time comes he should still be around because you never know when a helping hand might be needed.

A word of caution — the Yamaha Safe Rider Training Course, as well as many experienced teachers, specify a motorcycle no larger than 100cc for training the beginning rider. This may not be practical in individual cases, but it is strongly recommended.

Having started the bike, it is time to disengage the clutch and shift into first gear by pressing the gear lever. The clutch should be released very slowly, while gradually increasing the throttle. It takes practice to do this smoothly, and the practice should be done on a wide open space, like a vacant parking lot or a large yard where there is nothing to run into. The trick is smoothness. Shifting is practically a lost art for automobile drivers in an age of automatic transmissions. The technique of shifting, mastered properly, can give you a fine sense of accomplishment.

Once in first gear the best exercise is to practice riding in a straight line at low speed for short distances, say 20 to 50 feet. Ride a short distance, pull on the clutch, and use the footbrake to bring the bike to a full stop. It is difficult to balance yourself while going slowly, much more so at 5 to 10 mph than at 20 to 30. Don't be in a hurry to go fast. Slow first-gear riding is important to master. To make sure you are concentrating on a straight line

Right side lever (left) is the front brake, left side, the clutch.

and not wiggling all over the place, half out of control, practice riding toward your friend. The idea that he is keeping an eye on you will make you concentrate harder. He should remind you to keep your head up and eyes looking straight ahead, rather than down at the ground just ahead of the front wheel. Looking down is an easy habit to develop, and a bad one. Also, if he is directly in your path, his presence will make you practice using the brake. If you are going as slow as you are supposed to, there is no danger of hitting him, but in case of a problem, he should have plenty of room to back up and lots of space to move laterally, one way or another.

After coming to a stop, using the foot brake and disengaging the clutch, practice backshifting into neutral. Cultivate the habit of dropping into neutral and putting a foot down every time you come to a full stop.

The next exercise should also be done in first gear. With a friend standing in a stationary position make slow, even circles around him. This gives you a feel of the amount of lean it takes to turn a certain radius. After a few laps, turn and go in the other direction.

Now you're ready to work on shifting. Concentrating on the smooth application of both the clutch and the accelerator, ride in a straight line, shift up to second, brake, shift back down to first, then continue a short distance, brake, and after a full stop shift into neutral. Stopping, shifting up and down, and stopping again does wonders for developing coordination. Continue the shifting exercise up through the gears. The braking effect of engine compression will become quite apparent as you shift down, and you will learn how to slow the bike almost to a stop without using the brakes at all.

Merely knowing how to shift up and down and how to lean into a turn are not enough to familiarize the beginning rider with the potential usefulness of his machine. At this point it would be a good time to take a leaf from the Yamaha Basic Rider Training Course. At about the third lesson the instructor lines up a set of cones and has his students zigzag through them at low speed, left, right, left, right. Rocks or just about anything can be substituted for cones — tin cans, bricks, bottles. They should be placed fairly far apart at first, and after you find this easy to do, move them closer together.

Playing on an obstacle course which you can arrange any way it suits you, as long as it is level and has nothing solid to run into, has plenty of challenging situations and is not only fun but very instructional. While practicing on the course, be sure to have plenty of opportunities to practice braking. If you get tired of one layout, rearrange it. There is no such thing as too much practice.

When you feel confident enough during this period, gradually begin to use the front brake along with the rear brake, being careful to use them only when traveling in a

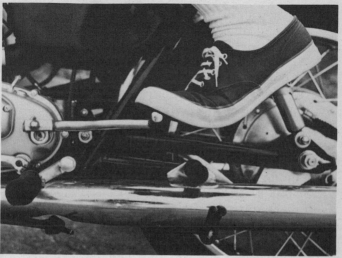

straight line. Use them lightly at first until you get the feel of how the bike handles under front and rear braking.

After eight hours of this sort of riding, everything should feel more natural. You should have conquered the tendency toward jackrabbit starts, which are not only bad for equipment but potentially dangerous to the rider. You should understand about keeping the revs up in all gears to keep from lugging the engine. You should have practiced shifting into neutral every time you come to a full stop so that the procedure is automatic. You should be able to shift so smoothly up or down that the bike does not lurch. Now you're ready for the hardest part of all.

Cecil Zaun, a retired driving safety official for the Los Angeles City School System, once quoted a statistic we have never forgotten. He said that of 1500 motorcycle riders killed in 1967, 75 percent were riding rented or borrowed motorcycles. The implications are that (1) these riders didn't know their machines and (2) many really didn't know how to ride.

The point is this. All the familiarization in the world won't guarantee your safety out there where automobiles and trucks rule the streets and highways, and where a large number of drivers resent your taking up part of the space they feel entitled to. What you have equipped yourself with in this do-it-yourself motorcycle riding school is to handle the motorcycle smoothly and automatically. It's important that you do not have to stop and think every time you want to turn, shift, or brake. It's important that you develop an ear for shift points so that you don't daydream down the street, lugging the motor so badly that it won't respond when you suddenly wake up and need it to do something quickly.

Having become acquainted with the motorbike, you are aware without anyone lecturing you that it is uniquely safety-oriented in comparison with an automobile. A motorcycle takes up a tiny space and is very maneuverable, which can be a tremendous advantage in a tight situation. You have 360-degree visibility with no steel barriers in any direction. In traffic you sit higher than the man driving a car, and you can see what is going on farther ahead than he. You can accelerate better than anything on the road. If your bike is 250cc or less you can outbrake anything as well; big bikes have relatively the same stopping distance requirements as automobiles.

On the other hand, while riding a motorcycle you are barely, if at all, visible to the motorist, and everything you do on the street has to begin with the assumption he simply can't see you. Should you have a collision with a car, you are in deep trouble, because there is no doubt of the outcome of any scrap between a 4000-pound automobile and a 250-pound motorcycle. Your ability to stop quicker than a car puts you in double jeopardy, because you can avoid the sudden emergency situation up ahead oftentimes only at the risk of being run over from behind.

There is a third hazard in traffic, and it has to do with the incredibly bad driving habits of some motorists. While you are tooling down the street, trying to stay out of everybody's way, you never know when you are going to encounter a zombie at the wheel, a drunk, or some psychologically disturbed individual who has it in for all motorcycle riders. We hate to mention this, but we reported a murder story for a newspaper once in which an enraged motorist actually chased a motorcycle rider with his gun blazing. He finally killed the bike rider.

So before rolling down the driveway into the street in front of the house to fetch a magazine at the drugstore, try to commit these universally accepted safety tips to memory:

1 *All the motor vehicle laws that apply to automobiles also are in force for motorcycles.* Drivers often take liberties with the law, but motorcyclists don't dare. Drivers coast through boulevard stops with their automatic transmission, but motorcycle riders have to stop, put their foot down, and proceed. Anytime a bike guy breaks, cracks, or even bends a traffic ordinance, he runs the risk of alienating someone in a 4000-pound automobile.

2 *Assume you're the invisible man.* Nobody can see you at any time. It's not far from the truth. A motorcyclist makes a small image in the rearview mirror, or otherwise traffic officers wouldn't be able to sneak up on lawbreakers so easily. Once you take it for granted you can't be seen, then you begin to practice real, honest-to-goodness, defensive riding. That's the right way.

3 *Pay attention to the surface on which you are riding.* Particularly keep an eye out for *changes* in the surface. The cyclist's biggest nemesis is the pothole. Where the pavement ends and the dirt detour begins, slow down and be careful or you'll be likely to spill. In many residential areas the cross streets bring with them gutters that crease the street you are riding on. In a car that gutter means

76

a nasty bump, but on a motorcycle if you are not careful it means an airborne trip into a nearby tree. It is impossible to monitor the roadway if you are tailgating the car in front; so back off and give him room. Leave even more room if you are being tailgated because you are risking the chance that the fellow up front will slam on his brakes and turn you into a motorcycle sandwich.

4 *Railroad tracks need to be crossed perpendicularly, never at an angle.* Take it slowly as well. The same applies to streetcar tracks, where they exist.

5 *Avoid wet streets, rain, ice and snow.* If it's raining, park. Even motorcycle police don't go out in the rain on their bikes — they switch to patrol cars. In the event you approach a place where there is water in the street, slow down and proceed very carefully. If the water is deep, don't take chances; something might be hidden under the surface. Detour if at all possible. Water can be negotiated, but lots of skill is usually required. On country roads water and ice are often found on the inside of curves. The best way to handle them is to slow down and ride through patches of danger in a straight line. That means entering and leaving the turn as widely as safety permits and cutting to the inside.

6 *Look out for moving obstacles.* When George Tirebiter, the dog, chases a car, all he gets is the smell of the tires, but the part he likes best about the motorcycle is your leg. The temptation is to kick old George, but that just gives him a better shot at it and doesn't help you keep your balance. Well-practiced pooches even lead the motorcycle so that they can stay with it longer. The best thing is not to let them disturb you but to speed up and try to get out of range as quickly as possible. There is another type of moving hazard: the occasional child or pet who dashes out into the street in front of you. The only way to avoid this hazard is to plan ahead — keep an eye out for small people and animals as you ride down the street. Be particularly wary of ball games because the old rule still applies: A bouncing ball is always followed by a running boy. If the ball goes into the street, so will the boy.

7 *Beware of all cars making a turn, particularly a left turn.* This is a common cause of accidents, and a particularly tragic cause for the motorcyclist. The man turning left is trying to judge the oncoming traffic, and if he doesn't see the motorcyclist, he leaves that part out of his estimate. The best way to know when he is going to make a turn is to watch his face (is he looking at you, for

example?) and his arms. The steering wheel can't move until they do. Meanwhile, slow down and prepare to use the brakes.

8 *Beware of all parked cars.* Imagine you're invisible to the man about to pull out into traffic. He's supposed to stick his head out the window and see if the way is clear, but nine times out of ten he won't. He may use his sideview mirror, but what if you don't show up in it? Keep an eye out for any car that has someone sitting in it. There is always the possibility someone will step out on the street side. A good number of motorcycle accidents involve the rider running into an opened car door.

9 *When riding in traffic, stay just to the left or right of the center of the lane.* The center is all slick with oil dropped by automobiles, but there are always two tracks where the wheels have picked up the oil and left a clean pathway.

10 *Driveways represent a special hazard.* Cars backing out of them usually can't see you and won't stop to let you by. Drivers turning into them seldom bother to use their turn signals — they're home, you see, and they have switched off their "obey the traffic laws" computer already. In a residential area, when following a car, give him plenty of room, and when he slows down, get ready. He

may turn left or right into one of those driveways up ahead. You'll never know till he does it.

11 *Don't squeeze past cars in the "extra" lane that is wide enough for your bike but not for a car.* You take a chance on lighting that anti-motorcycle fuse for one thing. For another, you are a sitting duck for a lane-changer, a guy who accidentally moves over on you and catches a handlebar (that probably means good-bye), a fellow who forgot to signal he was going to make a turn at the next corner, or a traffic officer.

12 *Slow down at night.* Road conditions are even more difficult to spot in the dark. The rule of thumb is never overdrive your headlight.

13 *Give a car plenty of room when passing him or when he is passing you.* The reasons are obvious. He can do a lot more damage than you can.

14 *Be prepared for anything.* Once some ghoul stretched piano wire neck high across a heavily used motorcycle trail near Saugus, California. It was an almost invisible guillotine. Fortunately, the first rider who came along was alert. He thought he saw something and stopped. The wire hit him but only resulted in minor injury. Low branches can knock a rider clear off his bike the

same way they did in old movies. Only when you do it instead of a Hollywood stuntman, it isn't funny.

15 *Be extremely careful about looking back.* Remember that at 40 mph if you look back for one second you will travel 59 feet before you face front again. Safety experts say it takes 44 feet at that speed to react to an emergency situation and another 88 feet to get stopped.

16 *Don't be distracted.* The advertising people who put up those billboards intended them for the fellow sitting in his air-conditioned sedan with power everything who is bored to death and welcomes a change of scenery every now and then. Even more tempting are the young, beautiful girls found strolling in every major city. We don't want to discourage girlwatching, but would recommend if there is something interesting enough to look at, stop and look, then proceed.

It is said that off-road riding is a lot safer because of the absence of cars, trucks, buses, children running into the street, and many of the other hazards we have just listed; but safety is a relative thing. You're just as bad off lying in the weeds with a broken shoulder, next to a mangled bike, 35 miles from the nearest house, as you would be if you were struck down at First and Main by a tank truck.

Let's go into some of the potential hazards of off-road riding:

1 *The very pleasure of off-road riding, aloneness in the wilderness, is also its main hazard.* Riding alone is asking for trouble. In fact desert races are set up so that patrols move in behind the competitors and literally "sweep" the landscape looking for fallen cyclists. An experienced desert rider will light a fire to signal his whereabouts. That can be a dangerous practice because of the hazard of brush and forest fires. So the best protection you can have is a buddy to ride along with you.

2 *Train yourself to expect the unexpected.* Even when traveling over familiar ground, be ready for anything. When you look out over a beautiful prairie it looks as smooth as glass, but when you ride over it you find out differently. After a little experience you get to know that what will cause an accident the easiest is what you can't see. Rocks and low fences hide in the tall grass. Sheer dropoffs are just around the next corner. Hikers are a half-mile up the trail, and while they can hear you coming closer they might not know just when you are coming around the bend. Birds and insects can be expected to make random kamikaze dives at your face shield. Frightened animals may run into your path or in an extreme case launch an attack. Abandoned mine shafts and excavations are everywhere.

A smart rider demonstrates the safe way to cross railroad tracks (or any other irregularity in road surface)—perpendicular to the tracks, regardless of the direction of the road.

3 *Know where you are welcome and where you are not.* More and more open land is closing to motorcycle recreation. The reason is that bike riders before you have abused their welcome, and now farmers and householders take it out on you. They retaliate by calling the law and in some cases by taking the law into their own hands — with guns.

4 *Ride with knees hugging the fuel tank and feet on the pegs.* The temptation is to relax in the seat and let the knees hang out. The easiest way to fall off is to sit this way and let the feet dangle. It's a good way to break a leg as well. All good off-road riders lift their bottoms off the seat and come to a nearly standing up position. They can see better and they are ready for anything. They can get a

better feel of what the bike is doing and can steer better. And they aren't risking compressed vertebrae every time the motorcycle bounces off a rock.

5 *Be careful with water.* Water hides things, just as grass does. If you fall off and lose consciousness in the dirt, you might be all right in a few minutes, but it would be tragic to do it in a brook and drown in six inches of water. When your bike goes down in the water, the abrupt temperature change could ruin your engine, leaving you not only with a costly repair bill but stranded to boot. In shallow water the footing sometimes changes rapidly from a rock-lined bottom to soft mud or sand. Catch a front wheel in that and over you go, usually head first.

6 *Sand takes special technique.* You have to get moving fast enough not to bog down (the faster the bike travels, the higher it rides), but slow enough to keep on the lookout for hazards.

7 *Hill climbing.* It's great fun to ride up a hill, because most off-road bikes can climb almost anything, with enough of a run at it. You lean forward, hit the throttle, and soon you're up and over. There are two problems: stalling on the way up and what do you do when you get to the top. If something makes you stop on the way up, don't let the bike roll backwards

under any circumstances. Drop it and get off. You might have to pick the machine up in pieces later but at least you'll be able to pick it up. There's another funny thing about hills. They always have another side, the one that goes down. If you hit the summit at 20 or 25 mph and there is a drop-off, what are you going to do? The best practice is to slow immediately at the crest to look the situation over for the downward run.

8 *Riding downhill.* Take it slow and easy, in a lower gear. Forget the front brake on a steep descent, unless you like to play leapfrog with 150 to 250 pounds of iron. Practice with shallow hills first to build up your confidence, then work your way up to the bigger ones. The most serious trouble you can have is an out-of-control ride down a steep, bumpy hill. There is no way to get off or away from the bike without serious injury. Just hang on and ride it out.

9 *Practice using the front brake at low speeds on level ground until you feel confident about handling the bike.* Always remember the front brake works a lot better than the rear brake, a phenomenon that makes the wheels want to swap ends if braking isn't a smooth, coordinated motion. After a while, practice using them together until it comes naturally.

10 *On narrow, twisting trails keep the feet up on the pegs.* Never stick a foot out in a turn over rough terrain. It could catch hold of something and pull you right off the bike. What is caught could easily break.

11 *Learn to use the bike in every way — it can get you out of trouble.* That means learning to do "wheelies" and how to jump properly.

A word about wheelstands or "wheelies": You may think of them as something to do to show off, but they have a definite function in off-road riding. The rider who knows how to ride balanced on his rear wheel can avoid many obstacles, such as rocks and fallen trees. With the front wheel in the air, all the shock is absorbed by the rear wheel and rear suspension. Directional stability is hardly affected at all.

The best place to practice wheelies is on an almost level but slightly uphill slope. While riding in first gear at low speed, stand up, lean forward, and lift the handlebars firmly while giving a slight twist to the throttle. To prevent flipping over backwards, keep your foot on the brake pedal and be prepared to use it. Application of the rear brake brings the front wheel down. The most common mistake of new riders practicing wheelies is trying to do too much too soon. Don't try to see how high you can go. Just take things nice and easy. Otherwise you'll have a crippled piece of machinery and maybe a few injuries of your own to show for your efforts. Should the motorcycle loop on you, try to get off running so you won't be underneath when it comes down. When bailing out, be sure to let go of the handlebars and move laterally away from the bike.

Now about flying through the air: When approaching a jump you should be standing up on the footpegs, because you will need all the strength in your two legs to absorb in the impact upon landing. Don't reduce power until you're in the air, then hit the throttle upon landing to keep the rear wheel from landing too hard. The most important thing is to keep the front wheel higher than the rear wheel, because if the front wheel lands first, you're in serious trouble. Although you cut the power while in the air, a blip of the throttle will assure you the engine is still working.

In all of the previous, concerning both street and off-road riding, it cannot be stressed enough that the machine should be kept in perfect running condition. Tires should be inflated to recommended pressures, fuel should be checked, the electrical system should be in good order, and the engine properly serviced. It is also a good habit to go over the bike and tighten all the bolts every time you take it out. A little later in the book we will turn the subject of maintenance over to a real expert.

4. Survival Is No Laughing Matter

The average motorcyclist has a median age of twenty-two and rides 3000 to 5000 miles a year, mostly for recreation. He carries a passenger about one-fourth of the time, lets other members of his family use his bike 5 percent of the time, and lends it to others to ride about 5 percent of his annual mileage.

The accident rate per unit distance traveled is slightly higher for a motorcycle than it is for a car, but the fatality rate is five times higher. Our average motorcyclist would be most likely to have his accident during the first six months he was riding. One-half of all motorcycle accidents involve riders with less than two years of experience.

In any motorcycle accident there is a high probability that a serious injury or fatality will result. The most common injury is to the head, which happens 150 percent more frequently than a leg injury and three times more often than an arm injury. The rider is almost always thrown off his bike in an accident. Those are the conclusions of a study conducted for the National Highway Safety

Bureau by the Transportation Research Department of Airborne Instruments Laboratory in Deer Park, New York. There are probably later studies available, but this one covers the period of greatest growth in the use of motorcycles in the history of the United States, 1949 to 1966.

The most important fact brought out by the analysis is that motorcycle riders have improved their record for traffic safety in the face of tremendous growth in the use of this type of vehicle.

In 1949 there were 31 million registered motor vehicles in the United States. By 1966 the population of automobiles, trucks, and buses had more than tripled to 96 million. In the same period motorcycles increased in registration from 197,920 to an estimated 1.8 million, or nine times as many.

Fatal motor accidents involving drivers, passengers, or pedestrians increased 71 percent from 31,701 to 53,000, while during the same period motorcycle fatalities jumped 95 percent from 1103 in 1949 to 2160 in 1966.

Traffic fatality figures are tragic, of course, but the fatal motorcycle accident cloud has a silver lining. The research group at Airborne Instruments Laboratories found that fatalities per 10,000 motor vehicles on the road inched downward in that period from 7.09 in 1949 to 5.52 in 1966. At the same time the motorcycle fatality rate plummeted from a high of 23.03 to 11.28.

In other words, the risk a motorcyclist takes

in getting hurt is still greater than the chances for a fellow who sits surrounded by all that steel in a sedan, but compared to the way things used to be when the risk was three times as great, definite progress has been made. One of the reasons for improvement of the record is that the everyday motorcyclist today is more likely to be a young, vital person with good reflexes, better than average eyesight, and a healthy body that heals more easily.

The Airborne Instruments Laboratory study pointed out that 58 percent of motor vehicle drivers — and this group includes 90 percent of all persons in the United States over the age of sixteen — are male. By comparison, 93 percent of all motorcycle riders are male. According to the survey, the educational level of the motorcycle rider is higher, and since 35 percent of all motorcycle riders are under the age of twenty, the researchers concluded they had better eyesight and were in better overall physical condition.

A. D. Little, writing in "The State of the Art of Traffic Safety" for the Automobile Manufacturers Association, declared that driver error causes 80 to 90 percent of all motor vehicle accidents. In other words, nearly all traffic accidents can be prevented. For the sake of the motorcycle rider involved they must be prevented, because the odds of his coming out alive can be incredibly poor.

Once the relatively simple skill of riding is mastered, the rider must learn how to stay out of trouble. Operating a motorcycle has the effect of making a better citizen of the road out of a rider, because the motorcyclist is compelled to work harder at his practice of safety than anybody else.

It can be done. The California Highway Patrol reports that its motorcycle officers cover 8 million miles a year at the cost of 175 accidents. That amounts to one accident for every 45,000 miles under the most unfavorable conditions possible.

What are some of the serious problems that can confront a lone rider suddenly without warning? What should be done about them?

1 *Debris in the street.* Whenever traffic allows, the best thing to do is to stop and clean it off the roadway. If you run over something big or sharp enough, stop and check for tire or rim damage. Wire in the street can get wrapped into the spokes of a wheel or into the chain and cause a sudden stop. At the first suspicion of this, stop immediately and make an inspection. Check tires regularly for nails and broken glass.

2 *Objects that fall off cars.* If something looks loose and ready to fall, try to signal the driver about it. If he pays no attention, either stop and let him put some distance between you, or pass him and let the piece of his car drop where it won't do you any harm.

3 *Gravel, dirt, and mud.* When such foreign matter projects out onto a highway from a construction site, for instance, it is a hazard that could cause your wheels to slide out from under you. Detour if you can or slow down and pick your way through. If it's really bad, stop.

4 *Median strips.* Stay away from both the concrete islands and the painted double lines, which are slick as glass. The same applies wherever a highway has an expansion joint in the center of the pavement.

5 *When you have to ride in the rain.* Wait fifteen or twenty minutes after it has started raining. This gives the rain time to clean oil and dirt off the surface of the pavement. If it is only drizzling, wait even longer.

6 *You are riding down the highway and suddenly a gust of wind hits you, knocking you off balance.* It wouldn't do that if you were paying attention to local weather conditions and the terrain. You can get socked with a gust of wind when you come out from behind a hill. Be braced for that. The effect can be just the same when you come out of the wind and go behind a hill. Compensating for a crosswind has made you lean into the breeze, and you have to stop leaning the instant you feel the wind stop.

7 *A dip in the road is ahead.* The one place you don't want to get airborne is on the highway. Slow down and take a good look at what's in the bottom from the entrance to the dip. It could be flooded, or there could be an accident or a stalled car blocking the road in there. You won't know until you look, and when you look you need to be going slow enough to stop if necessary.

8 *You are purring along a dirt road just below the foothills of a mountain range, and suddenly a washout looms ahead.* You are traveling too fast. The washout shouldn't surprise you, because you are paralleling the mountains, and you should not have to be told that every spring of water runs down the mountains, not up.

9 *Approaching a signal.* Anticipate the amber (yellow) light. Don't try to speed up to beat the red unless the car behind you is tailgating and you have no choice. The one time you speed through the intersection, that will be the time Joe Dragster jumps the signal and collects you for a hood ornament.

10 *Sitting at the signal.* Don't leave the bike in gear. It should be in neutral. In first, with the clutch out, is the time the clutch cable might pick to break. The result could send you hurtling into the path of the cross traffic.

11 *Sitting at a boulevard stop with a car approaching from one side.* Wait long enough to see what he is going to do. He probably doesn't see you, and he may be in the habit of running that stop sign regularly. Let him go.

12 *You are truly the invisible man.* One way to improve the visibility situation is to use the headlight all the time, day or night. Some states require this. Many police departments burn headlights as a standard procedure. Even long-haul buses do it.

13 *When taillights flash on ahead on the freeway.* Begin slowing immediately, before the chain of lights reaches the car in front of you. Keep tabs on the car behind you, which could scoop you up if conditions were right. Signal him by using the turn signals, left, right, left, right. Always look for someplace to get out of the way. That's why the fastest and slowest lanes are the best places to be. They offer convenient escape areas.

14 *A car decides to change lanes and occupy your space.* Back off or speed up, whichever is safest. But don't argue, move.

15 *In the country, a farmer pulls out of a side road directly into your path; there's no room to stop.* You have acceleration. If you see him coming, use it to get by

him. If there is no traffic coming, use all the road you need to, but stay away from him. He's an accident looking for someplace to happen.

16 *You are starting to pass a car, and up ahead you see an obstruction blocking his lane.* Back off if you can. If you can't, move as far to the left as possible. Just figure automatically that he doesn't know you are there and will take evasive action — into your lane.

17 *You and your buddies are riding in the desert, very close together, when you go down in front of them.* Stay down and don't move until they get past or stop. At this point they can maneuver a lot quicker than you can. It would be a shame to get up and run into somebody's path after escaping injury in a fall.

18 *Cresting a hill.* Stay to the right. An automobile coming from the other direction will crowd the center line, anticipating a right- or a left-hand turn on the other side of the hill.

19 *Overtaking another motorcyclist.* Do it cautiously, giving him plenty of room. At highway speeds his rearview mirror may be vibrating so badly it is useless. He can't hear you because of the wind. If you come upon him too quickly, you will surprise him, and he may react by losing control. Sammy Tanner's rule of

thumb is never pass anybody on the road more than 10 mph faster than he is going.

20 *When - the throttle sticks.* Pull in the clutch lever, brake, and kill the ignition. Get stopped. If the problem is dirt in the linkage, you can probably correct, it. If not, park the bike until repairs can be made.

21 *Speed wobble.* There are many causes, but when the wobblies get you, the cause is academic. Accelerate quickly to get the weight off the front wheel. Hit the rear brake only, stop, and get off. Check for a loose axle bolt, and check the steering dampener.

22 *Rounding a curve on a gravel road, you feel the rear wheel start to lose traction.* Turn the front wheel in the direction of the slide. That will keep the bike upright. Back off the throttle and dirt track it around. If you start to go down, don't hit the brakes. Put your foot out to slide on. Once the bike goes down, let go and push off. Get away from it.

23 *The sun is low, and alternate groves of trees cast dark shadows across the road between patches of bright light in the open spaces.* Visibility has deteriorated. Slow down. Your eyes are fighting it.

24 *The road is straight, the traffic is light, and your mind is beginning to wander.*

That is the first sign of road fatigue. You're lucky in a sense you are not in an old car that allows carbon monoxide to seep through the floor boards, making the driver even sleepier than you are. Avoid highway hypnosis by stopping about once an hour. Walk around, have a smoke, or drink a cup of coffee. Break the monotony.

25 *A large bug chooses your face shield for a ticket to Heaven, splat!* Train yourself not to panic and not to take your hands off the handlebars. As soon as you can, stop and wipe the shield as clean as possible. Congratulate yourself for wearing eye protection. At the first sign of a rest room or water pump, stop and clean the shield thoroughly.

26 *You know you are going to crash into a wall or tree.* Lay the bike down. Locking the foot brake helps bring the rear wheel around. Try to do it as soon as possible, because there is still a chance you will slide into the tree, along with the machine, if you are going fast enough when you land.

27 *You have crashed, and you took a sharp rap on the head.* Inspect the helmet for damage. If there is a scratch on the outside, there is a good chance of damage on the inside, where you can't see it. Do what the racers all do. Return it to the manufacturer for inspection.

various views of motocross racing

Leaping over an obstacle.

Stuck in the mud and out of the race.

The mass start at Hopetown, California.

Three riders duel through a turn.

Wrestling a motocross bike around a tight turn in the soft dirt.

There is no catalog of specific recommendations to cover every situation you will face. The foregoing are offered as guidelines, but what they amount to is common sense. In catastrophic situations, there is nothing to do but cast your lot with fate. Under identical circumstances one fellow will stand up, brush himself off, and walk over to look at his crumpled machinery, while another will never move again.

The really serious rider will practice leaving his bike, laying it down at low speed to get the hang of it. A course in tumbling never did anyone any harm. Athletes who either have or who develop great coordination and dexterity have an advantage, particularly football players who are coached "how to fall." Why is it one fellow goes through life falling off ladders and walking under descending flower pots without suffering anything more than a bruise and a cut or two, while another poor soul finds a banana peel on the sidewalk and cracks his skull, or walks into a revolving door and fractures his leg once every six months? Call it chance or fate or luck. There may be more to it than that. We've seen the same youngsters hurt playing football too many times, while others who have taken harder knocks keep playing year after year with no time lost due to injuries.

How do you apply this to safety on motorcycles? First, you adopt a "stay out of trouble" attitude, avoiding situations you know you might have trouble handling. That means slowing down for corners and letting the pushy guy in the GTO cut in front of you on Woodward Avenue, and it means riding across the desert at moderate speed, expecting to find trouble and not making like J. N. Roberts in the Mint 400. Second, you think about the tough problems you just barely avoided and try to analyze what you would have done if...Third, you practice simple things like laying the bike down, taking pains to do it at slow speed on a soft surface so you won't hurt your equipment or yourself. The experienced racer, by the way, leaves his bike with his head down, protected by his shoulders. Fourth, you try to work yourself into the best physical shape possible.

Did you ever look closely at professional motorcycle riders? There is hardly a pound of blubber among one hundred of them. The best pros are lean and muscular. They have to be to maintain the stamina and take the body punishment that racing demands. Ask any rider, and he'll probably tell you he doesn't work out at a gym or play handball or jog. He just rides a lot, and that keeps him in shape. One thing is certain, he didn't start racing motorcycles out of condition.

The Airborne Instruments Laboratory safety study declared that the average rider puts 3000 to 5000 miles of wear on his bike every year, compared with 9000 to 12,000 for the average automobile driver. But what the safety researchers didn't break down was the mileage each person drove or rode purely for pleasure, and the mileage covered because he had to. We suspect the ratio would have been reversed, with maybe 2000 miles of motorcycle riding for fun every year and less than half of that for automobile recreation.

What this implies when placed next to the accident statistics is that the motorcycle jockey is out having fun and hurting himself more often than the motorist, who is mostly driving back and forth to work or school. That's an exaggeration, but it means something to a cautious rider who is interested in keeping his head intact and his bones in one piece. It means you don't take your mind off what you are doing while riding a motorcycle for one second. It means you don't take your mind off what the other people are doing around you, not for one second. It means more than defensive driving. It means, "Think survival."

A Word About Protective Clothing

We mentioned earlier the importance of the safety helmet, proper footwear, and gloves. The helmet is an essential, because it can mean the difference between life and death in even the simplest of accidents. We knew of a beautiful young lady who was a national kart racing champion as a teenager. She won two hundred trophies in the course of a few years, traveling around the country with her father and brother. At the age of eighteen and recently married, she won a race that had as first prize a small-bore motorcycle. On her first time aboard, one-half block from her home, she was riding the new machine at 5 mph when she had an accident, hit her head against a utility pole, and was killed.

This young woman was not unfamiliar with crash helmets. She had worn one from the time she was thirteen years old, but for some reason she failed to wear one that fateful day. Here was virtually a professional racer, who had thousands of miles of competition behind her, but she was careless. Her father claimed her life would have been saved by the helmet she left at home.

A salesman we know sold a bike to a fellow who was short of cash. He tried but couldn't sell the customer a helmet. Two months later the customer came in and bought the helmet. On the way home a car turned in front of him, and the rider went sailing headfirst over the hood. He stood up, dusted himself off, and rode back to the dealership.

"I just wanted to say thanks," he said to the salesman.

It has taken a while for the word to get around about foot protection, as well as helmets. Our library includes safety books and pamphlets that show riders without head protection and wearing a variety of footwear from sandals and high heels to loafers, ballet slippers, and tennis shoes. The most startling photograph of all shows a father on a mini-

Lace-up shoes or boots are the most highly recommended footwear for motorcycle riders. Lace-up boots are preferable to pull-over boots because in the event of an injury they can be removed more painlessly.

bike giving a ride to his son, who is balancing sidesaddle on the fuel tank in front of pop, and his daughter, who is riding on his shoulders. There isn't a helmet in the bunch.

For street riding, ordinary leather shoes are acceptable, but lace-up boots are recommended. A compromise is the pull-over boot, the zip-up boot, or high-top shoe, because they give ankle protection. Off the road, nothing but a lace-up boot is recommended.

The ideal body protection, of course, is the leather suit, which costs anywhere from $50 to $150. Keeping in mind that after a head injury the most likely part of the body to need protection is the leg followed by the arm, a set of leathers is a good investment. In lieu of leathers, the next best protection is full-body coverage, that is, long pants and a long-sleeved shirt, preferably covered by a jacket, sweater, or other outer garment. T-shirts, short pants, miniskirts, bathing suits, and hot pants are stylish, but they beg for trouble on a motorcycle.

A lady who really went looking for trouble was the attractive young woman who was first seen in the vicinity of York Boulevard and San Pasqual Street in the Highland Park district of Los Angeles, early in the morning on April 30, 1952, wearing nothing but goose pimples. The Los Angeles Police Department unit which first spotted her was eagerly joined in pursuit of the carefree cyclist by other police from Pasadena and South Pasadena. She lost them a couple of miles away after a chase that was described on the police blotter as "enthusiastic."

The problem with lecturing about the proper clothing is that the manufacturers' advertising doesn't always agree with what they preach in their safety literature. In a typical month's issue of a popular motorcycle magazine we found ads showing a blond wearing knee high pull-over boots and hot pants, a brunette in white boots, hose, and a two-piece sports outfit that exposed most of her legs, a woman in a miniskirt, and a hatless young man on a bike displaying his colorful and proper street jacket. That's Madison Avenue for you.

Carrying Passengers

See the nice daddy.
He rides a motorcycle.
Ride, daddy, ride.
Look at Johnny.
Johnny is with daddy.
He holds onto daddy.
Smart Johnny.
Daddy is smart too.
He wears a helmet.
If daddy falls off, he won't hurt his head.
What if Johnny falls off?
Johnny has no helmet.
Daddy is not so smart after all.

How many times do we see the young motorcyclist riding down the boulevard, fully covered from helmet to proper boots, with his scantily clad girlfriend clinging to him? Some smart guy. He is just as bad as the father who gives the kid a ride on the motorbike without equipping him with at least as much protection as he knows he must have.

Passengers need the same protection against injury that the rider does, and they need a few words of caution as well. Riding double is a whole new game. Let's think about it for a minute.

1 *The handling geometry is drastically altered by a passenger.* Take a 250-pound motorcycle, add a 150-pound male, and the total is 400 pounds, but add a 110-

pound female and suddenly it's up to 510. That's asking a lot, even of a finely crafted piece of machinery. The weight, however, is not nearly so critical as where you put it. It has to go over the rear wheel, because that is where the extra sitting room is. Suddenly there is more strain on the rear shocks, more weight up high altering the center of gravity, more load for the tires, wheels, and spokes, more pull for the engine, and less efficient steering because the front end is lighter.

2 *Braking efficiency is lowered.* More weight means more inertia. Not only is the rolling mass more difficult to stop, but any sudden need to stop means the motorcycle stops quicker than the two people it is carrying. Your passenger will be pushing forward against you in an emergency with possibly disastrous results.

3 *Turning can be an adventure.* Unless the passenger is practiced enough to let you do the leaning and not fight against you or try to help and thereby lean too much, you will find cornering much more unstable. Tell the passenger to let you do the work and just go along for the ride. The best place for him/her to lean is onto you.

4 *Where do the extra feet go?* Not all bikes have an extra set of footpegs. To carry a

passenger, make sure yours does. Tell the person in the back seat to keep their feet up on the pegs when you come to a stop and put your foot down. It's difficult enough balancing the extra poundage without having to fight a wiggle worm. As for youngsters, the very young can't reach adult footpegs. Build on a set just right for those little ones who ride with you. It's not hard to do.

5 *Panic.* "Ho, ho, ho! I'm sure scaring her." Those could be nice words for an epitaph. The frightened passenger wants off, now, and might do just anything. You could both go down, or he/she could "step off" at 40 or 50 mph with predictably terrible consequences.

Riding double can be enjoyable, but safety is important. Note that both the operator and passenger are wearing head, eye, arm and leg protection. The woman is holding the operator around the middle, which is the safest way to hold on. Riding double is not for beginners. It requires special precautions and the use of common sense.

6 *Steep climbs.* Don't try them. You're asking for a fatal accident. We've already lived through that mistake, thankfully. The weight is too far back on the rear wheel for the bike to get proper traction up a steep hill. Leaning forward helps, but usually not enough.

7 *Holding on.* One answer is to install a buddy bar, but the best method is a locked hand grip around the middle, as long as it isn't a death grip that squeezes the wind out of the operator.

There is nothing amusing about a motorcycle accident, particularly one with more than one rider on a single bike. Riding double is no time to do tricks, race, or clown, because the punch line to the joke could be grim.

In 1952 the Road Research Laboratory of Great Britain worked out a scale on danger for the known forms of transportation. Motorcycles topped the "risk of death" scale at a magnitude of 40. Next came bicycles at 14, airplanes at 7, automobiles at 1, trains at 0.2, and passenger ships at a fraction so small it was called "negligible."

5. Simple Owner Maintenance

In 1962 Bill Krause was an auto racing driver with a great future. He had won the prestigious Los Angeles Times Grand Prix at Riverside, California. He had been Carroll Shelby's first test driver for the Cobra, and he had been one of General Motors' first test drivers for the Corvette Sting Ray. He had gone to the Indianapolis Speedway to drive in the "500" for Mickey Thompson and had been offered a chance to race a Formula 1 car in Europe.

With a small nest egg he had put away from his race winnings and income he had earned working long, hard hours, Krause bought a franchise to sell Honda motorcycles, and he turned his back on what was considered at the time to be one of the most promising careers in motor racing. Starting in a 1400-square-foot building with one employee, he built one of the nation's most successful motorcycle dealerships. The motorcycle business was as fast-growing then as it is today, but very few people could have predicted then the tremendous potential of the sport of

motorcycling — a potential on which Bill Krause and others in the industry have built their fortunes.

Today Bill Krause has forty-nine employees in a complex that covers 20,000 square feet — almost half a city block — in Inglewood, California. Bill Krause Enterprises, Inc., the parent company, manufactures and markets motorcycle accessories and operates Bill Krause Sportcycles, a dealership which sells Honda, Triumph, and Yamaha motorcycles. The Krause service department has been called by many in the industry the finest retail service facility in America, and it is certainly at least one of the best. It is a showplace. Because of his reputation for good service and his experience as an instructor and a lecturer, we called on Bill Krause of Bill Krause Sportcycles, Inglewood, California, to contribute this chapter on owner-maintenance of the motorcycle:

Rider maintenance can save many expensive trips to the local dealer for major re-

111

pairs. Quite often these repairs would not have been necessary if the proper owner service had been performed.

Before we discuss the details of rider service, I think it would be in keeping to give a brief description of the differences between motorcycles or sportcycles and the more familiar automobile. The first and most obvious differences are the size and the lack of two wheels which render the bike unable to stand by itself without some sort of prop. While these are easy to recognize, there are many less noticeable to the inexperienced layman. Some of the more pertinent yet often overlooked characteristics are related to the comparatively small displacement of the engine. Also motorcycle engines, with few exceptions, are air-cooled. Most beginners start on small one- or two-cylinder models ranging from 60 to 125cc which, after a few weeks of getting used to, are usually run at maximum speed and throttle opening. The latter may cause a relatively new rider some exciting problems when riding a friend's large cycle for the first time. Due to these conditions, and the small amount of lubricant carried, it is imperative to maintain proper oil levels and use the best lubricants available.

Items requiring frequent checking are the control cables, rear chain, and oil level. Motorcycle engines vary with regard to the number of cylinders including the now famous three-cylinder models which seemed impossible to build only a few short years ago. There are, however, really two basic types: the more traditional 4-cycle model and the now equally popular 2-cycle model. In order to understand the differences in these engines, it is important not to confuse the word cycle with the word cylinder as they are totally separate entities.

First let us briefly explore the 2-cycle engine. While 2-cycle engines may vary as to cylinder arrangements, the principles remain basically the same. The 2-cycle engine fires each time the piston reaches the top of the stroke or, more accurately, a few degrees before top dead center. The principle does not allow time for valves as used in 4-cycle engines to operate before the next power stroke. This enables the 2-cycle engine to have a simple cylinder head design which is really just a cap for the cylinder containing the spark plug and providing a combustion chamber with external cooling fins. As you

Most motorcycles come equipped with a small tool kit. Be careful when using other tools, since American wrenches, based on inches, often do not fit foreign nuts based on the decimal system.

can see, this type of engine has no conventional valves to adjust, and therefore, it is a simple design requiring few adjustments.

Most 2-cycle engines used in motorcycles are of the piston port type, which means the piston actually performs the job of any other piston and also acts as the valve controlling the air-fuel mixture both on intake and exhaust. Some manufacturers prefer to use the rotary valve system on most of their 2-cycle engines, while others, such as Yamaha, only use this principle on engines of small displacement. A rotary valve is usually a rotating flat disc with sections removed to allow the air-fuel mixture to enter at specific times, thus providing a more positive control. While this is an advantage from a technical point of view it also requires some maintenance and often leads to the carburetor being mounted on the side of the crankcase. This can be somewhat clumsy in appearance and the extra width may interfere with trail riding.

The one thing all 2-cycle engines have in common is the lack of lubricant stored in the crankcase, as the incoming air-fuel mixture must pass through here prior to being transferred into the cylinders. This in turn means the engine must get its lubricant with the fuel by the pre-mix method or through a total loss oil system. These systems meter to the engine minute, but adequate, oil which is consumed along with the fuel. One of the most common problems with new or very old 2-cycle engines is that the oil supply exceeds the ratio

Rear drive chain should be inspected regularly according to instructions in the owner's manual.

Chain is tightened by loosening the axle nut and then using adjuster screws at the rear of the swing arms.

tolerable by the spark plug causing a fouled plug condition. This can usually be remedied by using a spark plug having a hotter heat range than would normally be recommended, or by reducing the normal lubricant. Be sure to solicit expert advice before attempting to make such a change, as serious engine damage may result if proper precautions are not taken.

As we have previously mentioned, due to the design characteristics of the 2-cycle engine, oil or lubricant is passed through the engine and out the exhaust pipe or muffler. These engines therefore require periodic cleaning of the exhaust system. Most current 2-cycle motorcycles used for street or a combination of street and off-road use have an oil injection system which automatically meters oil into the engine. In this case the basic responsibilities of the owner are using the correct type of lubricants and diligent checking of the oil reservoir.

A critical thing on 2-cycle engines is to maintain the proper ignition timing and point gap. This will minimize the possibility of excessive heating and help assure maximum performance. While timing is a relatively simple thing, it must be done with good equipment and careful attention. This adjustment should normally be performed only by an expert or after counseling by a professional. While there may be many variations in these engines the basic principles as explained here are the common denominators.

Spokes also need constant attention. Bill Krause recommends checking the spokes by spinning the wheel free and listening for a ring. If only a few are loose, they can be tightened by a "non-expert," but if most or all of them are loose, it is wise to have a pro do the job.

The generally accepted rule of thumb is that 2-cycles lend themselves better to off-road use while the conventional 4-cycle is more widely accepted for touring.

While 4-cycle engines as applied to motorcycles are much the same as those used in the automobile, they must perform at greater efficiency per cubic inch.

The Japanese have pioneered production of overhead cam engines of small to medium sizes which are designed to operate at very high rpm. These engines produce unusually high horsepower relative to their size. Other than the various cylinder arrangements these engines also vary in the placement of the camshaft, which is the heart of the valve mechanism. Motorcycle camshafts, as in automobiles, are often reworked by hop-up enthusiasts seeking more power. There are two basic locations for the camshaft, either in the crankcase using cam followers and pushrods to reach the valves, or in the cylinder head itself. As we previously mentioned, all modern Japanese 4-cycle engines have them located in the cylinder head, while most English cycles use the pushrod system. The most popular arrangement, used in Japanese cycles, consists of a single camshaft with a rocker arm for each valve. These rocker arms have an adjusting screw for setting valve clearances, which needs periodic checking.

Now that you have a basic understanding of the two types of powerplants used in modern motorcycles, you will find that the controls and chassis of most cycles are basically the same.

If you happen to be the proud owner of your first motorcycle, it is important to study the owners manual before attempting any adjustments. Whether you have a new or used cycle, one of the best ways to detect problems before they become serious is to keep it clean. Keeping your bike clean will naturally enhance its value and encourage your pride of ownership as well. Because of the many exposed parts on a motorcycle, it is more complicated to clean and more vulnerable to damage as a result of carelessness. It is best to use a soft rag to remove mild road dirt and normal contamination. If excess dirt or mud has collected, it will require washing with water and a mild detergent. Extra caution must be used when rinsing your bike to prevent damage to air filters and contamination of oil reservoirs and carburetors. Many cycles have been damaged extensively by well-meaning but uninformed sons or daughters who cleaned Dad's bike. One such example might be filling the exhaust pipe and subsequently the engine with water. After washing with water be sure to dry the exterior and run the engine as soon as possible, both to prevent moisture from entering the engine and to circulate the lubricants. The painted and chrome parts should never be cleaned with an abrasive; a good paste wax offers the best general protection for these items. Many of the aluminum cases are coat-

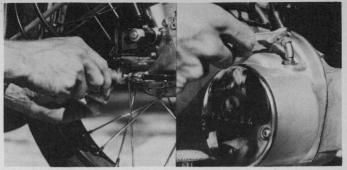

Rider adjusts brakes,   clutch cable,

handlebars   and front shock absorbers.

Checking and adjusting bolts and other parts of the motor-cycles should become a routine for the bike owner.

ed with a clear lacquer. Care should be taken not to remove this, as it will result in oxidizing of the exposed surfaces.

With few exceptions, sportcycles are equipped at the factory with small but adequate tool boxes and tool kits. These tools are designed to encourage owner maintenance and allow emergency repairs to be handled by the rider. Since most motorcycles sold in the United States are imported, it is seldom that American wrenches will do a proper job.

There are three basic bolt size designations used throughout the world, the American fractional sizes, the English Whitworth sizes, and the metric system. The metric system is currently in use by most countries, with the exception of British Territories and the United States. It is important not to try to mix any combination of these, even though a few can be interchanged, as permanent thread damage may result. Remember the old adage, "Don't put a square peg in a round hole."

Providing you now have a brief understanding of owner maintenance, here are a few of the operations that can be performed using the tools supplied with the cycle.

It would first be wise to check your owner's manual to see if it is the correct one for your cycle. If you find you do not have the correct manual, it would be well worth your effort to obtain one from your local dealer or distributor. The owners manual usually has a page or two describing the tools supplied with the cycle for your comparison.

Before you start off on your cycle you should always check all cables and controls for proper adjustment. Most cable adjustments can be easily made at the control by turning the cable housing receptacle in or out for proper free-play.

Rear drive chain adjustment is normally controlled by the position of the rear axle. It is necessary to loosen the axle nut or nuts before attempting to tighten the chain by using the adjuster screws at the rear of the swing arms. After making the adjustment to the chain be sure to check the rear brake free-play as this will be affected by moving the wheel. Installation of an oversize rear tire may require additional chain links or a half link to provide adequate tire clearance. This brings to mind the importance of maintaining the recommended tire pressures which are of extreme importance on a motorcycle. The handling, safety, and tire life are directly related to tire pressure and terrain. Another important item related to tires and safety is the tightness of the spokes. This can easily be checked by spinning the wheel while holding a metal object against the spokes. Spokes having the proper adjustment should have a slight "ring" as they make contact with the metal. If only a few spokes are loose, they may be tightened to achieve the same tone as the others. If all or most of the spokes are loose, the wheel should be removed and re-trued by a professional.

In order to have the reliability we all expect from our cycles, there are certain things we take for granted on our automobiles which require watching on a motorcycle. Because of the greater heat generated in the cylinder heads of air-cooled engines, and other related factors, spark plug life is greatly reduced. The average life for plugs on most touring bikes is from 1500 to 3000 miles. When checking the plugs, it is also possible to determine whether the engine is running too rich or too lean. Excess oil deposits may reveal such things as bad piston rings. Spark plugs which have a light gray or white color around the center electrode would indicate a lean condition. A black smudgy look would normally be due to an overrich condition which may be caused by a wet or dirty air filter. For air cleaner maintenance it will be necessary to refer to the owners manual as there are too many different types to go into here.

Because of the limited space and weight factors on motorcycles, batteries have limited storage for electrolyte and require frequent attention to liquid level. Most Japanese batteries have a clear plastic case with fluid level lines for easy checking, and they are usually located under the seat.

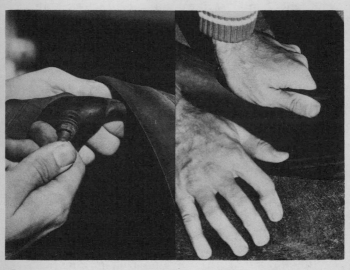

Careful attention must be paid to motorcycle tires. A rider inspects the valve to find stem damage (left) which is terminal. He looks at the tire casing to check for damage after a particularly bad jolt (right).

A simple thing like dirty ignition points will cause an otherwise perfect cycle to become inoperable. If you are not experienced enough to set the point clearance, it is a simple job to clean them with contact cleaner and get your cycle running.

One of the best investments you can make, if you intend to do your own maintenance, is an impact screwdriver. This is necessary to remove the cross head screws which are installed at the factory with power tools. The heads of these screws are usually ruined when trying to remove them for the first time with an ordinary screwdriver.

If you are an off-road rider only, the information contained herein would also apply to you. However, special attention should be given to items such as air cleaners, fork seals, spokes, and chains. Riding in the high desert or mountains may require changing to a smaller main jet for peak performance. A word of caution, however, don't forget to change back to normal jetting when returning to lower elevations. Please remember that a louder motorcycle is not necessarily a faster motorcycle. When in doubt, always refer to your owners manual instead of asking your buddy. With a little owner maintenance, your cycle should give many miles of trouble-free riding with only occasional visits to the professional bike doctor.

6. Safety, Ecology, Law, and the Cyclist

The consumer revolution in America began innocently enough with the quiet settlement of a lawsuit by General Motors Corporation over the issue of whether the Corvair was or was not inherently a safe automobile. Word of the out-of-court settlement leaked out. Bill Huddy, news director of television station KEYT in Santa Barbara, California, where the plaintiff lived, revealed it to the world one night.

Lawsuits of that type are usually settled with the understanding that the person who filed the action will take the money and keep his mouth shut. The winners often sign a legal document agreeing to keep quiet or give back the money. For some reason, this procedure wasn't followed.

Soon came Ralph Nader and his book, *Unsafe at Any Speed.* The automobile, symbol of American affluence, started coming under critical examination. Accident statistics suddenly assumed political importance. Junkyards filled with car bodies became eyesores to the public which had once ignored them.

Air pollution acquired new importance as a menace to public health. Some politicians attacked the internal combustion engine as one of the chief sources of peril in modern society. It is important to know the background that led to a new attitude toward "protective" legislation in order to understand governmental scrutiny of the role of the motorcycle today.

Even in a free society we all welcome some government control. Without it there would be chaos. Imagine riding down a street on either side, with no stop signals at the cross streets, oncoming traffic weaving its way toward you, no hand or blinker signals to warn you of sudden moves by the other fellow, and no policeman to take charge in the event of an accident. That would be totally disastrous.

By and large motorcyclists have accepted traffic regulations as a necessary part of the scheme of things. What alarms many of them is the sudden attention lawmakers are paying to other aspects of the sport of motorcycling. Let's look at the legal side of motorcycling, especially the more modern trends:

Safety

Traffic enforcement and accident investigation officials have been viewing the motorcycle situation with alarm for years, particularly since the postwar boom has introduced so many new riders into street traffic. Work toward defining the problems and seeking solutions has intensified under the National Highway Traffic Safety Administration of the U.S. Department of Transportation. Riders can take some solace in the fact that the NHTSA's chief executive, Douglas Toms, is a motorcycle enthusiast himself.

Gradually, however, a pattern is emerging that indicates the motorcycle rider of the future will have to put up with more and more control. The federal government and many states are trying to set up uniform licensing standards and to start some kind of systematic training. So far, the state of Minnesota has the only worthwhile educational program, but it is only about as thorough as the usual high school driver education course. The student is taught how to ride safely, but he isn't instructed as thoroughly as he might be about the possibly catastrophic situations he may face later on. Whatever training program is finally agreed upon by all fifty states, nobody quarrels with the idea of having one.

There is, however, controversy over so-called compulsory helmet laws. So far, only seven states (California, Illinois, Iowa, Mississippi, Montana, Nevada, and Wyoming) have no law at all. While New Mexico requires helmets on all passengers and all riders under eighteen years of age, Kansas' law applies only to operators and passengers over twenty-one, and Utah applies its regulation only to those public roads where speeds exceed 35 mph. The Utah statute was tested in its State Supreme Court, which found that injuries to a motorcyclist are a matter of public concern.

Justice A. H. Ellett wrote in part of his majority opinion: "Both hospitals and relief rolls are crowded. Any measure which would protect the operator of a motorcycle would tend to avoid collisions with other traffic on the highway."

He somewhat confused a safety device intended to work during a collision with the actual avoidance of that collision, but he touched upon a tender subject with the tax-paying public — that the lone motorcyclist does more than endanger himself when he goes without head protection. He risks the expenditure of public funds to care for him in the event of an accident. In that way he theoretically represents a menace to society unless he is made to conform.

Justice J. Allan Crocket dissented, writing: "If the conclusion is based upon the possibility that cyclists may become hospitalized, or go on welfare, that opens a wide door indeed to paternalistic controls over innumerable aspects of human conduct as to what may or may not be good for one's individual health, morals or safety."

The safety helmet manufacturers also are not all four-square for mandatory helmet laws, believe it or not. One prominent manufacturer offered the opinion that mandatory laws would be bad for the industry, because they tend to encourage the starting of fly-by-night companies which jump in when the demand is high, market inferior products, and then drop out when demand falls, leaving the good companies weakened. Meanwhile, thousands of motorcycle riders would (under this line of reasoning) be wearing helmets which do not meet rigid safety standards, and they would have a false sense of security.

The motorcycle industry lobby in California pulled off an interesting stunt to make its point about the mandatory helmet law. State legislators were all issued safety helmets and asked to wear them for a day. The uncomfortable representatives of the people quickly disposed of the bill by burying it in a committee. There are an estimated 1.5 million motorcycles registered and unregistered (off-road) in the state. That amounts to something between 20 to 25 percent of all the motorcycles in this country. A California helmet law would have had a profound effect on both helmet and motorcycle industries.

The fact remains that with forty-three of the fifty states requiring helmets and an increasingly protective attitude by government officials, it may be only a question of time before helmets are strapped on to avoid traffic citations everywhere in the Unites States.

Twenty-eight states currently have laws requiring eye protection for the motorcyclist, although two of them — Michigan and Washington — only require goggles or face masks at speeds above 35 mph, and Utah's statute applies at any speed on a road with a speed limit over 35. Those states which have no law requiring eye protection are Alabama, Cali-

This fellow is asking for trouble. He parked his motorcycle in a space too small for a car, but he is close enough to take a hit from the Chevy in front or the VW behind—or both when they pull out.

fornia, Idaho, Indiana, Iowa, Kansas, Maine, Massachusetts, Minnesota, Mississippi, Missouri, Montana, Nebraska, Nevada, North Carolina, North Dakota, Oregon, South Dakota, Texas, and Wyoming.

Licensing remains the biggest single factor in efforts to improve motorcycle safety. Few states have a stiff examination, and only thirty-six have any special license or testing procedure for motorcycle operators at all. We went to a California Department of Motor Vehicles office to get a book and bone up for the motorcycle exam one day. The licensing examiner had to apologize and state that he had never seen one. We called another office, and the woman who answered the phone said that of course there was such a book, but she had been out of them for several months. They were on order and were expected any day now.

Despite the fact that many states have been lax in the licensing department, it is only a matter of time before there will be some form of licensing everywhere in the U.S. Just as the licensing requirements for automobile drivers have varied all these years, there will probably never be standardization unless the federal government steps in. And don't think that might not happen!

Not all states have laws affecting passengers on a motorcycle, rearview mirrors, and other safety-oriented regulations. Twenty-nine states have some form of safety inspection, either at the time the motorcycle is licensed or more frequently. Some states either have laws or interpretations of other safety regulations that inhibit the builders of so-called "choppers," the homemade hot rods of two-wheeling.

Noise

At the time this is being written there are twenty-two separate motorcycle noise abatement bills in the legislative hopper in California, where much of the pioneering is done as far as motor vehicle law is concerned. As a practical matter, only one or two of them have a chance to be enacted, but the number of proposed statutes — and the number of different lawmakers who have proposed them — is a good indication of the mood of the public on the subject of excessively noisy motorcycles.

In California, where the standards are at least as strict as they are anywhere else currently, Section 23130 of the Motor Vehicle Code allows a maximum of 82 decibels for a machine traveling 35 mph or less, and a maximum of 86 for a bike traveling more than 35 mph, unless it is defined as a "motor-driven cycle." Decibel levels for that type of bike are restricted to 76 dbA at 35 mph or less, and 82 dbA above 35.

Russ Sanford, the motorcycle enthusiast's only paid lobbyist, reports that the trend in new legislation is to reduce decibel levels. He points out that another provision of the Motor Vehicle Code, Section 27160, requires manufacturers to comply with a diminishing noise level depending on the year of manufacture. These are the maximum decibel levels allowed by law in California:

Motorcycle manufactured before January 1, 1970 92

Motorcycle manufactured after January 1, 1970, and before
January 1, 1973 88

Motorcycle manufactured on or after January 1, 1973 86

Motor-driven cycle manufactured after January 1, 1968,
and before January 1, 1973 86

Motor-driven cycle manufactured on or after January 1, 1973 84

What this means is that the owner of a 92-decibel motorcycle is expected to maintain it in 92-decibel condition. It also implies that all owners of motorcycles in California had better know how loud their street machines sound, because they may receive traffic citations. Not only that, but 7 of the 22 proposals in Sacramento would revise the present standards to an even quieter level.

California has another law, Section 27150 of the Motor Vehicle Code, which requires a muffler on all registered motorcycles and leaves the enforcement of a provision against "unusual or excessive noise" pretty much up to the officer on the street. Sanford claims that this section has nailed many motorcyclists, who have been convicted in court even though their bikes met the requirements of Section 23130 (noise standards they must maintain) and and Section 27160 (noise standards manufacturers must conform to).

Laws like this, which undoubtedly exist in other states, leave the motorcycle rider at the mercy of curbstone justice. In California, one of the twenty-two bills in the hopper is designed to eliminate the injustice of the "unusual or excessive noise" rule. It would require that the California Highway Patrol conduct scientific tests upon which reasonable standards would be set in line with economic and engineering facts. Once these standards are established, if the bill becomes law, it would then be necessary for a police officer to prove scientifically that the motorcycle was too noisy rather than to stand there and listen to it and decide for himself.

It is certainly reasonable that noise standards be set and maintained on public streets and highways. Particularly in cities, traffic noise is said to be a contributing factor to poor mental health. Ecologists are now telling us that the same harmful effects of loud noise apply as well to wildlife. Excessive noise frightens animals and sometimes "disorients" them, that is, confuses them and makes them forget where they are or what they were just about to do. It doesn't take too much imagination to predict that noise standards will be applied to off-road motorcycles in the near future. Bills to do just that have already been introduced in the California legislature, and one has passed.

The new law extends Section 27150 (the "unusual or excessive noise" law) to all off-road vehicles. The legislator who introduced it admitted he erred and has already proposed an amendment that would make the test of "unusual or excessive noise" any decibel level above those required for motorcycle manufacturers (Section 27160).

Both to conform with the new noise laws and also to live up to what are considered to be broad public responsibilities, the motorcycle industry is attacking the noise problem in its own way. On the retail level dealers will not sell an unmuffled motorcycle manufactured after December 1971. They coach their salesmen to do everything they can to discourage the sale of unmuffled expansion chambers and megaphones. At the factory level research is going on that will soon enable production motorcycles to put out maximum horsepower with the muffler intact. In addition, a new bike owner who tampers with his muffler risks having his warranty voided. At the racing level many clubs and associations require bikes with expansion chambers to be muffled as a condition of each entry.

The concept that wilderness areas are just as spoiled by noise as by littering, carelessness with fire, indiscriminate real estate development, plundering of natural resources, and emission of water and air pollution is a new one, but it makes some sense. Rather than being unfairly restrictive of motorcycle activity, however, noise legislation for off-the-road vehicles will probably turn out to be a routine matter that riders will learn to live with. To enjoy the privilege of riding in areas where no other human sets foot, or at least where no other vehicles can travel, it is going to be necessary for motorcyclists to observe some simple restraints.

Ecology

It used to be called conservation. In school we all studied about how the loggers and the oil drillers and the gold miners literally ripped apart some of the richest and most beautiful land in the United States to extract minerals, water power, and lumber. To be in favor of conservation and against exploitation was something every youngster learned to do, but few were ever in a position to practice.

Today's ecologists give us all a guilty conscience. We are all to be blamed for damaging our environment by creating pollution, by littering, by allowing bad planning of suburban and rural areas and poor zoning practices in the cities, by our wanton destruction of plant and animal life, and poor population planning. We can no longer blame only the big corporations for ruining our scenic open country. Every one of us is just as much at fault.

The off-road vehicle enthusiast is a conve-

Ecologists are down on off-road riders partly because of the way some of them litter. Unfortunately, not all motorcyclists are careful about where they dump their trash. Thoughtlessness such as this has made it tough on all off-road riders and has lined up hard-core ecologists against the sport of motorcycling.

nient scapegoat for the ecologist and some cyclists deserve it. While the motorcyclist doesn't choke the seashore with tons of crude petroleum from leaking offshore drilling sites, he does occasionally start brush fires because his bike is not equipped with a spark arrester. He does leave litter behind. Some thoughtless riders rip through virgin brush country, crushing tender plants, or deliberately killing small animals and birds. Ecologists sensitive to the delicate balance of nature would rather motorcycles not be allowed in places where they could endanger the natural scheme of things.

As we pointed out before, noise pollution has become an important rallying point for those concerned with the preservation of other species of life on this planet. One of the early targets of ecologists was the snowmobile driver. Charging across the still, white countryside during hibernation periods of most animals, the snowmobilist was accused of waking and frightening the fauna of the land, disturbing their life cycles and threatening their extinction.

During other seasons the motorcyclist and the dune buggy driver are said to do almost the same thing. Therefore, there are those who would eliminate the sport of off-road motorcycling or at least severely restrict it. To preserve the right to ride in wilderness areas the motorcycle enthusiast must use good sense and restraint while moving about in nature's wonderland.

Encroachment

There is more than one use for open land. It is there not only to ride a motorcycle across. It attracts a great variety of nature loving people, who have many different reasons for being there. There are sportsmen, who hunt or fish. There are campers and hikers. There are prospectors and explorers. There are geologists and botanists. Some ranchers use public land to graze their livestock. There are homesteaders who either occupy the land to settle on it, to retire, or to make use of it as a vacation retreat. Most of them resent interference with their own personal pursuits.

Folks who fled to the country to "get away from it all" do not like to wake up in the morning to the sound of loud motorcycles. Ranchers get boiling mad when arrogant motorcyclists trespass on their land, sometimes leaving gates open or cutting their way through fences. Fishermen are perturbed when cyclists splash through streams and frighten fish away. Destruction of crops and stealing or killing livestock often makes the motorcyclist who had nothing to do with the original crime an innocent target of vengeful farmers armed with guns. Once we wrote in a newspaper column about the need for more motorcycle recreation areas to satisfy the needs of the off-road cyclist, and we were astounded by the amount of mail the column attracted — every letter against motorcycles. One retired gentleman who lives on a dirt road, where young riders travel on weekends en route to the back country, invited us to trade homes for a weekend to see how we liked the noise level he had to live with.

In California, the restriction of off-road motorcycling reached epidemic proportions in 1970, when four of the southern counties where most of the desert riding is done — Los Angeles, Orange, San Bernardino, and Riverside — passed ordinances forbidding a rider to use private land without the owner's permission. Many cities also adopted anti-motorcycle ordinances that were so strict that a youngster could not even ride a minibike on his own front lawn legally.

The issue of pro- and anti-motorcycling never came more clearly into focus than it did in the Bean Canyon case. Bean Canyon is a scenic wonderland near Bakersfield, California, laced with motorcycle trails that have been in use for more than twenty years. Riders used to come from all over the West to enjoy the area. There was never a complaint until two things happened. Roger Nichols, a songwriter for Herb Alpert, bought a parcel of land on top of a hill overlooking the canyon, and he began planning to build. Soon he became aware of the fact that motorcyclists were crisscrossing his property despite all the postings telling them to "keep out." One story goes that a fresh bike rider reached out and pinched Nichols's wife one day as she stood on her homesite. Meanwhile, the hillside was acquired by land speculators who subdivided it and began selling parcels to vacation home seekers and retired people. They were probably doing a far more damaging thing to the ecology of the area by cutting down trees and leveling building sites than the bike riders had by riding there, but salesmen objected strenuously to riders racketing back and forth, while they were trying to make their sales to elderly couples in search of a quiet mountain retreat.

One or more of the new property owners induced a local magistrate to take action against offending motorcyclists. So officers began appearing on the scene in January 1969. From then through April they stopped each rider, indicated they were taking a "survey," and wrote down the rider's name and address. Nearly everyone cooperated. Meanwhile, complaints were drawn up in April charging one hundred and fifty persons with violations of the state trespassing law, and these were served by mail in June and July. Many of the one hundred and fifty thought they were being cited for traffic violations and merely pleaded guilty. They were shocked to learn the fine was $65. Very few realized they were being charged with a misdemeanor for which they could serve time in jail. One rider wrote a letter to *Cycle News* telling of his predicament, and the letter brought response from many others who were charged with the same offense. An AMA District 37 official put the writer in touch with an enthusiastic Bakersfield motorcyclist who was a lawyer.

Attorney Ray Alan Yinger wound up representing sixty-five riders who had been served with the same complaint. All sixty-five cases were eventually dismissed on a legal technicality, which did not touch on the constitutional issue of the right of motorcyclists to use open land. Since October 1969, when the sixty-five cases were dismissed, California's trespass law has been tightened, and its validity has been upheld in lower courts. The law makes it a crime for a motor vehicle to be on private property without the owner's permission. Yinger and others believe the law has constitutional defects, but to date there has not been an appeal to test that theory.

Use of Public Land

The most enlightened government agency, from the point of view of the motorcycle enthusiast, is the Bureau of Land Management. The BLM, which for years has concerned itself mainly with administering the disposal of homestead land of the federal government, has suddenly found itself in the recreation business. The BLM administers 457 million acres of government land. The problem it has been asked to deal with is off-road vehicle use of open Western land under its control.

The concern is many-sided. Ranchers have grazing rights on some of the acreage. Ecologists are worried that off-road vehicles are permanently scarring the landscape. There are operators who indiscriminately drive wherever they please. Scientists complain that valuable fossils and archeological remains have been severely damaged by motorcycle, dune buggy, and ATV drivers. Particularly in California, where desert motorcycle riders have been legally pushed off nearly everything else, there has been pressure to use BLM land for off-road vehicle recreation.

So the BLM appointed a group of affected citizens called the Off-Road Vehicle Advisory Commitee (ORVAC) to study the problem. Its fifteen members represent ranchers, ecologists, the California Department of Fish and Game, and off-road vehicle users. Their main recommendation has already been put into effect.

ORVAC suggested that BLM land be classified into three uses. Class 1 is open, class 2 is restricted, and class 3 is closed. Open use means that just about anything goes. Motorcyclists may use restricted land, but they must first obtain a permit. Each permit application is to be judged on its merit. A restricted area might have a high wildlife population, or it may be classified as such to protect the cyclist from such unusual hazards as mine shafts and excavations. Areas are classified permanently closed to protect historic sites, fossils, and other priceless facets of the wilds in the West. It is sad to report that the great Indian Intaglios east of San Diego, California, have been all but destroyed by thoughtless and selfish off-road vehicle users.

The BLM has also recognized the so-called checkerboard problem which makes it impossible for riders to use vast areas under its control. There are many land owners in the desert, including the state, but more particularly the railroads, which acquired tremendous amounts of acreage years ago. Checkerboarding, a plan also practiced by ranchers, involves acquiring every other section (square mile) of land. This makes for an impossible situation as far as the motorcycle rider is concerned.

In most of the affected areas there are local ordinances forbidding off-road riding on private property without the owner's permission. Under these ordinances and the new California trespass law, many motorcyclists have been cited for riding on BLM land. The officer merely hands the citation over to the rider and leaves it up to him to prove to a judge whether or not he was on private property. That's next to impossible. There are very few surveyor's stakes in the California desert.

The BLM has already helped to alleviate this situation by opening the first of what may be many desert recreation areas. It is located in Stoddard Valley, just south of Barstow, California, on 12,000 acres of what is described as a motorcyclist's paradise. There is every type of terrain from flat valleys to mountains in the parcel.

Soon the BLM hopes to have the authority to carry out the next phase of its program, which is to go into the land swapping business. By exchanging acreage with the owners of desert checkerboards, the BLM would open additional recreation areas. A bill to implement this plan was introduced in the U.S. House of Representatives in July 1971, by Congressman Bob Mathias of Tulare, California, the two-time Olympic decathlon champion. Called the California Desert Management Act, it would give the BLM acquisition authority and establish a long-range program for management, development, and use of public land under the jurisdiction of the BLM.

There are two other government agencies which control public land: the U.S. Forest Service, and the National Park Service.

There are 154 forest areas and 18 grasslands with a total area of 81 million acres administered by the U.S. Forest Service. National forests are visited by 12 million campers every year.

Most of the forest areas are closed to all riding except that which is done on designated roads and trails. Recently, an experiment has been tried in the Los Padres National Forest near Santa Barbara, California, in which bike riders using U.S. Forest Service-approved spark arresters are allowed to ride anywhere on a particular 75-acre parcel. Riders are on their good behavior, because if the experiment is successful — that is, if the land is not damaged by carelessness or vandalism — it will be opened permanently, and perhaps other national forests will be opened to riders.

half-mile dirt racing
Ascot Park, Gardena, California

Ascot Park is the Mecca of motorcycle racers. Riders in a heat race are tightly bunched in the first turn.

Nineteen-year-old Keith Mashburn leans into a corner.

Head-on view of corner exiting technique. Note the various lines all four riders are taking, each trying to find the proper "bite" in the dirt for his machine.

The National Park Service has the strictest rules of all. It is charged with managing the priceless heritage of such natural wonders as Yellowstone, Brice, Zion, Yosemite, and Glacier National Parks. Under its jurisdiction are 32 national parks, 77 national monuments, 6 national seashores, and 4 national recreation areas, along with hundreds of historic sites. Riding in most parks is restricted to existing roads. Only in a few cases are motorcycles allowed on hiking and equestrian trails.

States have been slow to respond to the needs of their citizens for off-road vehicle recreation. Several have considered bills which would in effect license and register off-road vehicles and use the license revenue to acquire land and make improvements on it for motor vehicle recreation use. At this writing, none have been passed into law, but the chances of such an arrangement appear more likely every day.

The city of Los Angeles, which may have more motorcyclists than any other city in the world, has been particularly hard on off-road riding and has blocked several proposals to establish municipal riding areas. After closing an area near the black ghetto that had been used by youngsters on minibikes and small motorcycles for years, the City Recreation and Parks Department proposed in 1969 to open a riding area 30 miles north of the city near Newhall, California. The fact that poor minority children had been deprived of one more recreation opportunity and would be unable to take advantage of the new motorcycle park, if and when it was opened, apparently had little influence on the city officials. In all fairness, the riding area was closed in order to preserve a bird sanctuary. Two years after city officials promised motorcycle enthusiasts they would replace the closed area with a municipal recreation facility, there still was no bike park.

Meanwhile, in nearby Anaheim and Fullerton, California, two municipal riding areas were acquired by the recreation and park departments of those smaller cities, possibly the first two in the United States to provide its citizens with such facilities.

Into the void left by local government authorities, who have obviously either been reluctant to establish motorcycle parks, been unable to due to lack of funds, or simply haven't considered the problem, have jumped the private entrepreneurs.

In Southern California alone there are a dozen motorcycle recreation parks which have become known to enthusiasts all over the country — Saddleback Park, Claude Osteen Bike Park, Indian Dunes Park, Escape Country, Muntz Cycle Park, to name a few. Most of them feature both riding trails and competition areas where regular motocross, hillclimb, scrambles, and TT races are held. Expansion of the motorcycle recreation park business into a nationwide industry is easily predictable. In Japan, Honda already has a network of these parks, and the company has encouraged their establishment all over the world.

Air Pollution

Automobiles, trucks, and buses have been singled out for attention by the lawmakers who are sensitive to the public's growing concern about the quality of the air we breathe. In the war on smog, it is only a matter of time before they will turn their attention to motorcycles.

It is too early to predict what form of restrictions will be imposed on motorcycle users, but the inevitability of smog control is too important to ignore. It is true that it takes the exhaust of five or six 250cc motorcycles to equal the output of a Volkswagen, but there is exhaust, the exhaust is probably dirty, and eventually it will have to cleaned up by government action.

Theft

Theft of all motor vehicles is up to 20 percent in the United States, but theft of automobiles is down 27 percent. Obviously motorcycle owners are suffering. Motorcycles are being stolen at the rate of 150 per day. Insurance costs are rising even more rapidly than the rate of inflation, and even though higher rates are compensating for higher losses, insurance companies can't keep up with the thieves of today. Recently, in Massachusetts and New Jersey, the insurance companies were found to be paying out $2 for every $1 they were collecting. Other high loss states were Georgia, Nebraska, and Texas. Police officials estimate that today's motorcycle owner has about a 25 percent chance of getting his bike back if it is stolen. In addition to young joyriders, who account for a high percentage of all stolen vehicles, very highly organized professional theft rings are in operation in various parts of the country. The problem of preventing theft and reclaiming stolen motorcycles has reached such proportions that authorities have moved to do something to help the motorcycle owner.

Federal highway safety regulations call for every new motorcycle sold to have a Vehicle Identification Number. These can be successfully altered by the professional criminal, who typically forges a bogus registration for the stolen bike by using the registration for a crashed motorcycle that lies in a junkyard somewhere. But the day is coming soon when these numbers will be quite difficult to tamper with. The Society of Automotive Engineers has appointed a Committee on Vehicle Security to study the problem, and the National Auto Theft Bureau is also studying the special motorcycle problem. Proposals they have already suggested include making the numbering system easier to understand, placing serial numbers at various places on the bike, including inside the engine, and underlaying the Vehicle Identification Number with a grid that would be damaged if anyone tried to alter it.

The time is not far off when some new owner protection system will become standard for the United States and probably Canada as well. Today, using the present system, Vehicle Identification Numbers are transmitted throughout the United States and into Canada twenty-four hours after a theft.

Police report that their biggest headache in locating stolen motorcycles is the mistakes owners make in reporting their own numbers. Often it isn't their fault, because errors are made by clerks who record the registration papers and because some dealers are just plain sloppy. One California dealer was recently fined $750 for incorrectly reporting the serial numbers of 250 motorcycles he had sold.

It isn't much consolation to the motorcyclist who has just had his bike lifted, but legislation is on its way to help make it tougher for professionals to succeed in their illicit business. Meanwhile, it would be a good idea to look at the ways you can help prevent theft of your own machine:

1 *Try to park where you can keep an eye on it.* If that isn't possible, the bike should be parked where it is well lighted or where somebody else can watch it, such as a parking attendant.

2 *Always lock the bike.* That isn't 100 percent protection, but it usually slows the thief down, and if you make it tough enough for him, he may give up altogether. The best type is a steering lock but a padlock and chain wrapped around a solid object like a light standard or fence is also good insurance.

3 *Trick the thief.* Remove the spark plug and replace it with a non-working plug. Take an old, worn-out plug and deactivate it by breaking the electrode off the side. Put the phony in and carry the working plug away with you when you park. Or swap a dummy plug wire for the real one. You can often frustrate anyone but a seasoned pro by pulling tricks like these.

4 *Sound the alarm.* There are several good burglar alarms available, and you can rig your own by connecting the horn to the kick stand so that if the stand is disturbed, the horn goes off.

5 *Carry the Vehicle Identification Number.* It's too much to trust to memory, and often the only hope of recovering a motorcycle lies in quick reporting of the theft. Make sure, incidentally, that the number on the motorcycle registration is correct. Don't assume it is. Check the number.

Traffic Citations

No matter how careful a rider is, he may wind up in traffic court. Eighty-five percent of the time he will be guilty of some infraction and know it, 10 percent of the time he will be guilty of some violation of which he was ignorant until he collected the ticket, and the rest of the time he will be innocent.

Obviously, we are not interested in discussing the outcome of cases involving the guilty, even the "innocent" guilty who knew not what they did wrong until they got caught doing it. The law assumes everyone knows what is legal and what isn't. It is every citizen's responsiblity to make himself informed. Let's discuss what to do in the case of a wrongful citation, the one instance in twenty that should result in acquittal or dismissal.

The first thing to consider in defending yourself is whether or not to retain a lawyer. It's to be expected that the defendant in a minor traffic case will pay out more to an attorney than he will if he merely pleads guilty and pays his fine. One thing a lawyer can do, however, is advise the client how to appear in court and what procedures to follow if he is going to represent himself. American justice is supposed to work in favor of the accused until he is found guilty — and even after that, until he has exhausted every avenue of appeal. But once a traffic violation suspect gets into court he finds it doesn't always operate that way. A good attorney will help his client take advantage of every possible break under the rules of the court. He can advise when it is a good idea to enter a *nolo contendere* (no contest) plea rather than guilty or not guilty, whether to have a jury trial, what type of evidence to collect, which judge to avoid because of hostile attitudes, which judge to seek out because of his reputation for fairness, how to question an arresting officer when he is on the stand, how to ask for a continuance, and how to conduct one's self in front of the judge. In the case of the innocent, money for a lawyer is well spent, whether the attorney winds up making an actual court appearance or not.

The second thing to consider is the likelihood of perjury. All things being equal, a judge will be more likely to believe a police officer than a defendant, and the policeman knows that. It's only natural. However, the police officer approaches a court appearance somewhat differently from a man fighting a ticket. First of all, he probably had to come to court on his own time. That doesn't improve his humor any. Second, refusal to plead guilty is a challenge to his validity, possibly even to his honesty. That makes him grumpier and more determined to get a conviction. Third, it is impossible for every policeman to remember the details of every moving violation for which he writes a ticket. Some traffic officers deal out as many as twenty a day (even though they protest that there is no such thing as a quota system). To cover up for his lack of recall in comparison with that of the violator, who might remember the exact conversation between the two of them and have witnesses to back up his story, the policeman resorts to a pat sort of jargon, such as "I observed the defendant proceeding northbound in an erratic manner...." Quite often attempts to get a police officer to correct his story through questioning are futile even though he has made an obvious misstatement. He has been to court enough times to know how to handle himself. He is not likely to offer anything that would be helpful to the defense.

The third element of preparation for a court hearing is the gathering of all helpful evidence and testimony that will get the defendant's story across to the judge. It is important to be thorough and not overlook anything. Recall the exact place where the officer began clocking or observing the defendant. What was he doing just before that? Note traffic and weather conditions. Did he say anything out of line? Talk to possible witnesses. Drive by the area again and look for traffic signs. Are they hidden, hard to see, damaged? Take photographs to back up any story. One friend of ours pleaded innocent to traveling 45 mph in a 35-mile zone, then went on the stand to testify he was indeed traveling 45 — and won the case! First he went back to the place where he was stopped, along a route he traveled every day and knew well, and took motion pictures of the traffic flow at the exact time of day he had been ticketed. His movies proved that traffic was rushing by at 50 to 55 mph, and he managed to convince the judge that in traffic like that if he had gone any slower than 45 he would have been a hazard.

The fourth step is to pay careful attention to the presentation of the state's case. Take notes. The officer may make a misstatement or contradict himself. If the judge doesn't catch it, make sure you call it to his attention.

The fifth and perhaps the most important part of a successful defense is to make a good appearance before the judge. It may be surprising to learn that traffic court judges are pleased to hear an intelligent, logical defense and will lean sympathetically toward a person who is obviously sincere in his belief that he has been wronged. Judges, however, don't appreciate dirty clothes, skin, or hair, foul language or disrespect in any form. He can see through an obvious attempt to put something over on him. His experience has taught him that nearly everybody who appears before him in traffic court is guilty, and this experience has to make him skeptical of your defense whether he wants to be fair or not. If he catches a police officer in an obvious lie, he will probably give him a tongue lashing right there in the courtroom in front of you. Or if he doesn't like the way either case is presented, he'll probably say so. He will look upon a shoddy defense as wasting his time. It is not unusual for a policeman to be suspended for a short period if he traps himself in court in the act of lying about a traffic ticket. That can hurt the officer in the wallet, and it is even more reason why you can't expect to get a fair shake out of the police officer when you go to court against him and you are right. We know a fellow who learned this lesson. After being acquitted on an unfair traffic charge, he found himself being followed every day for three months by a traffic officer.

"You should have seen me," he said. "I was driving like a minister."

The traffic court judge sees himself as an instrument for traffic safety. He believes he acts as a deterrent to highway deaths by levying fines, suspending licenses, and ordering bad drivers to go to school. Maybe he does. At the very least he is entitled to the respect due a person who is trying to help society.

7. Two Wheels in Your Future

As far as motorcyclists are concerned, the year 1984 envisioned by George Orwell may get here sooner than expected. There seems to be little doubt that the government will take a more active part in control of the motorcycle by enforcing stricter safety, ecology, noise, and consumer protection standards. The National Highway Traffic Safety Administration is already moving to influence licensing practices. Various government agencies at every level, from the cities to the federal government, are making it harder for motorcyclists to go where they want to go off the road. Laws concerning excessive noise are a direct result of the bike manufacturers not moving quickly enough to do something about making their products quieter. Noise laws also have been influenced by irresponsible riders who purposely have magnified their exhaust sounds with expansion chambers and megaphones that someday may be outlawed.

Eventually, legislators may even feel compelled to enact a law requiring all brake controls to be located on the right side of the motorcycle and all gear selectors on the left. There are still a few manufacturers who persist in reversing the normal setup, a condition consumer advocates like Ralph Nader find incomprehensible. Their heads are filled with visions of the rider making a panic stop, hitting what he thinks is the brake lever, and shifting up into a higher gear instead. As we have all seen in recent years, government attitudes bend toward protecting the private citizen from his own folly.

New laws and their enforcement may take some of the fun out of motorcycling for its staunchest supporters, but there doesn't seem to be a limit to the expanding enthusiasm for the sport of motorcycle riding. No matter what happens to restrict enjoyment, there are apparently more and more people waiting in the wings to become interested in two-wheel recreation. The transition to a new era in motorcycle history has already taken place; in the words of Ivan Wagar, editor of *Cycle World*: "We don't have motorcyclists anymore. We have people riding motorcycles."

The love of motorcycles no longer sets the enthusiast apart from others in society. The bike lover may once have been seen as a strange, eccentric, maybe even undesirable person who refused to accept the realities of a four-wheel norm in this motorized world. "You meet the nicest people..." is an advertising slogan that literally made itself come true. Today's rider could just as easily be the boy or girl next door. He or she is definitely no longer just a kook.

That the future of the motorcycle is directly tied to social conditions in which more time is becoming available for leisure and recreation cannot be argued against. We have of course seen it happen in America, where recreational motorcycling has boomed during a period of ever increasing affluence. People have more time on their hands and more money to spend. There are more younger people capable of buying the things they want, and younger people are more adventurous, on the go and seeking thrills, less inhibited, less interested in comformity, healthier and more able to engage in physical activities.

Soon most American wage earners will have a four-day week. Some already do. Psychologists, sociologists, and urban planners are already worrying about what effect the new-found free time will have on the mental health of the four-day-week employee. What to do with leisure will be one of the important questions of future generations. The sport of motorcycle riding may play an important role in that future.

There appears to be a definite pattern of interest in motorcycles, as seen in their popularity here and in Japan, for example. Motorcycles competed with automobiles for acceptance as the best basic transportation in the early years of this century. The automobile, which offers more comfort and protection to the driver and his passengers, obviously won that competition. It wasn't until the Japanese manufacturers tried marketing the motorcycle as a recreation vehicle in the 1960's that sales figures zoomed upward in the United States. By contrast, Japan was selling motorcycles in its own country to people who needed basic transportation, and the marketing of transportation motorbikes was quite successful until the Japanese started making more money. Once they could afford automobiles, Japanese workers stopped buying motorcycles. Later, when Japanese manufacturers

A modern motorcycle production line shows the combined features of automation and thorough individual inspection.

started selling to their own people bikes intended for export, they were pleasantly startled at the enthusiastic response. These were recreation machines.

There are many areas of the world where people need better transportation but can't afford the cost of an automobile or the expense of maintaining one. Into these countries several motorcycle companies have gone with their products. It is too soon to tell, but it seems likely that two-wheel motor vehicles will become the rule in the lesser developed nations of the world in the next two decades, particularly in Southeast Asia and South America.

In highly developed societies, such as the one we have in the United States, it appears that traffic congestion may dictate a new transportation role for the motorcycle. One of the transport industry's more advanced thinkers, designer Alex Tremulis, sees a day when special lanes will be marked off on the freeways and expressways for motorcycles only. Lanes narrower than the ones where cars travel will allow faster transit for two-wheel commuters and remove much of the hazard of mixing automobiles and motorcycles from high speed travel. Tremulis goes further than that. He sees a design revolution ahead for the motorcycle industry.

The eccentric automobile stylist and designer who gave shape and advanced engineering ideas to the world's first safety car, the Tucker Torpedo, has long been associated

A view of the Honda factory.

with the idea that man can someday stabilize a two-wheel vehicle with a gyroscope to produce the ultimate in safety, maneuverability, and speed in an automobile. Tremulis was even associated with a project to perfect a "gyromobile" at one time, but it got bogged down in experimentation and eventually ran out of money.

Tremulis' Gyronaut X-1 Bonneville stream-line, ridden by Bob Leppan, was the forerunner of a series of Land Speed Record two-wheelers intended to be based on a gyro-stabilization. Gyronaut X-2 was to be the first two-wheeler with a gyroscope aboard to overcome the difficulty of getting a heavy vehicle from 0 to 100 mph quickly and decelerating to a stop. It would have been powered by a popular engine of the day, the 289-cubic-inch Ford Cobra, and had a design speed of 400 mph. This same two-wheeler powered by a fuel-burning supercharged hemi Chrysler, typical of the engines found in fuel-burning dragsters and funny cars, had a potential of 500 mph, according to the designer. Finally, Tremulis was ready to plunge the gyro-stabilized motorcycle into the unknown, beyond the speed of sound, with rocket power. Gyronaut X-3 was to weigh 3000 pounds, nearly half of which would consist of solid propellant. Firing three sets of rockets in sequence 5 seconds each for a total of 15 seconds at 9000 pounds thrust, the vehicle would be capable of covering a standing quarter-mile in 5.7 seconds and reaching 360 mph at the end of the quarter — or of streaking through the sound barrier and leaving it behind on the way to a maximum velocity near 1000 mph.

Due to the failure to date of anyone to produce a gyroscope system for a motor vehicle, none of this has happened. It is all in the mind of a somewhat practical dreamer, Tremulis. Why, you might ask, bother to go to Bonneville at all with such a radical two-wheeler?

The Gyronaut land record bikes were part of a grand scheme that could spearhead a revolution in the transportation sciences. The Bonneville runs were to demonstrate the efficiency of two-wheel transport for man. Single track vehicles offer many advantages over two-track automobiles. They are narrower and thus have better aerodynamics and fuel economy. They can be made smaller, lighter, lower, and longer (with gyrostabilization). They offer the stylist almost an unlimited range of shapes, whereas the four-wheel automobile is very restrictive to the designer.

Tremulis' imagination wandered over a new world of exciting challenge for the motorcycle builder. He foresaw trucks and buses on two wheels, army tanks, construction equipment, firefighting rigs that could travel almost vertically up steep mountain trails, lunar exploring cars, even commuter trains that could travel safely at speeds of more than 250 mph.

The one flaw in his plan was that the world still waits for someone to perfect a stabilizing gyro for an automobile. Once that is done, a safe vehicle must be guaranteed before the public will accept it. One of the more important questions left unanswered is: What happens to the gyroscope in a serious accident?

Returning to the practical world, which has no gyromobile, Tremulis still sees a new era approaching for the motorcycle industry, with exciting, radically different machines offered to enthusiasts in the near future.

"Look at the history of motorcycles," Tremulis said. "The motorcycle hasn't changed much since the beginning. It has had a very slow evolutionary development in comparison with the automobile. I believe the motorcycle is ready now for revolutionary change."

The motorcycle of the future, he predicted, is a three-wheeler with banking capabilities. Tremulis calls it a "poor man's gyrocycle."

The designer developed his concept around a curious looking "dream car" first proposed and patented in 1927 by the French designer Gabriel Voisin. It was diamond-shaped with four wheels in three separate tracks. Like a motorcycle, it had two main wheels fore and aft, and two side wheels served to stabilize it. This design enables the stylist to make use of the most efficient aerodynamic shape, the needle-nose configuration, and it suggested that head-on collisions might be reduced to minor bumps as the colliding pointed vehicles bounced off each other's sides. It also introduced the banking capability with which motorcyclists are so familiar but which is unknown in automobiles.

"I sometimes wonder," Tremulis commented, "if the future will ever catch up with the past."

From the Voisin diamond-shaped car, Tremulis evolved his Trigano. *Trigano* is a Greek word meaning "three points." The dream car as depicted by Tremulis is long and low, with seats for both the driver and the passengers side by side. They sit in automobile-type seats, rather than straddling a saddle. The most important feature of the Trigano is its banking ability, which Tremulis claims would make it a super stable vehicle, the perfect compromise between two- and four-wheel transport.

The Trigano would have the desirable features of needle-nose styling for cleaner aerodynamics, improved crash protection, and better fuel economy. It would have the ideal directional stability of a motorcycle, which is superior to any other class of motor vehicle in the world in maintaining a straight line. It would protect the passengers not only from the terrible G forces of head-on crash impact due to the pointed nose, but riders would be further shielded by an enclosing body. The unpleasantness (to many people) of the blast of air against the motorcyclist's body would be eliminated by the fully enclosed cockpit, and, of course, comfort would be greatly improved by bucket seats rather than the traditional saddle. Tremulis also claims that the elimination of placing the foot down to maintain stability at the parked position would be a great new plus factor for the three-wheel concept.

"A lot of people are hurt parking their motorcycles," he said. "Police especially have a significant injury rate caused by bikes falling on them."

In contrast to present three-wheel motorcycles and sidecars, Tremulis claimed the Trigano would be a very stable vehicle under a variety of conditions. The so-called dune-cycle, he said, is "the most dangerous vehicle in the world today" based on its unusual center of gravity and top-heaviness.

The "poor man's gyrocycle" would have a wheelbase more of automotive than of motorcycle dimensions, something over 100 inches. The stretched wheelbases of Bonneville streamliners, Tremulis claimed, support his premise that the longer the wheelbase the more stable a two-wheeler is in a straight line, and he claims that a banking three-wheeler is subject to the same design superiority a motorcycle has over an automobile.

To develop his theories about motorcycles of the future into something practical for the street today, Tremulis did a small-scale survey of several police departments in the vicinity of his Ventura, California, home. He found to his horror that motorcycle policemen averaged three trips to the hospital each year, and that in about one accident in four an officer could expect to suffer a serious injury. The three major causes of police accidents, according to Tremulis, were scrapes with automobiles, falling down, and high speed wobble. While the benefits of motorcycle use by police are well documented, the hazards are also well known. Most officers will not ride in the rain or join in a chase at speeds over 80 mph (they'll radio ahead and try to set up roadblocks). A flat tire while out in the field often requires the services of a truck and crew of three. Sirens operated by a rotor touching the front tire have a tendency to blow out the tire if they are started at more than 50 mph.

Tremulis' ideas on three-wheel bikes have been enthusiastically received by the police officials he has talked to. Whether or not motorcycle manufacturers will take seriously his proposals for a half-bike, half-auto like the Trigano remains for the future to be told. It seems clear, however, that motorcycles will become more civilized in the near future.

Industry observers make the following predictions:

(1) There will probably be retractable landing struts or wheels on motorbikes soon. They would be manually, electrically, or vacuum operated, possibly triggered by an on-board computer which signals the "training wheels" to lower or raise themselves at certain speeds or while the bike is at a standstill. The landing gear approach to holding a bike up while stopped at a signal, while starting the machine, or while parked would eliminate a good share of accidents and would permit motorcycles to be designed for more rider comfort. Keeping feet on the pegs or on a floorboard would be more than a comfort aid. It would give the rider more control.

(2) The sit-down seat will eventually re-

place the saddle. Purists who love motorcycles for the sheer enjoyment of having to
manage them — wrestling them around and
giving them commands like those a cowboy
conveys to his horse with the heel of his boot
— will probably object. But the more comfortable position offers many advantages. A comfortable rider is said to be better equipped to
look out for his own safety. His machine is
"idiot proofed."

(3) Stylists will change the bare bones appearance of today's motorcycles to futuristic,
bullet-like enclosed machines that will sit
very low to the ground. They will be popular,
low-price substitutes for sports cars.

(4) Eventually motorcycles will become as
quiet as automobiles, perhaps even quieter,
as the industry either takes leadership in
eliminating its noise problem or responds to
the prodding of the government.

(5) Three-wheelers with banking abilities
as high as 40 degrees will become the fastest
and safest machines on the street. Rocket
powered versions could set Land Speed
records approaching Mach 2 (about 1400
mph).

(6) Sophisticated running gear systems may
eventually replace the traditional chain
drive, just as the chain replaced the leather
belt of early motorcycles. The three-wheeler
will introduce such automotive niceties as the
differential and the automatic transmission.

(7) Wheels may become smaller as design
problems of setting the operator lower on his

bike are overcome, and brakes will of course improve.

(8) Multi-passenger vehicles will be made possible by the introduction of "training wheels" or gyrostabilization or some method of maintaining the two-wheel vehicle in an upright position when it is not in motion. Two-wheel trucks, buses, and trains are not flights of fancy. They could easily be built using today's technology. The problem remains: Who would buy them?

(9) Off-road riding will become more civilized, following a trend observed by knowledgeable people like Wagar. In the Northeastern United States, where cyclists are in the habit of riding woods and trail bikes and do not have a craze for speed, there are hundreds of miles of trails for them to use. They get along nicely with equestrians and hikers too. This is no accident. It resulted from a campaign spearheaded by Bob Hicks, publisher of *Cycle Sport*, and others. In the West, however, the noise, litter, destruction, and other side effects of uncontrolled off-road riding have taken their toll. It is almost too late for motorcyclists to negotiate for the use of riding space. The commercial motorcycle park takes care of some but not all of the demand. Motorcyclists will have to become more responsible and motorcycles more acceptable to the public at large or off-road riding will disappear.

(10) There will always be a motorcycle as we know it today. As long as there are free-

thinking, exploration-oriented men and women who enjoy the feel of wind against their bodies and enjoy mastery of a machine as personal as a motorcycle, there will be manufacturers willing to provide them. The motorbike does not seem destined to go the way of the horse and buggy.

A lone rider pauses to survey some of the wide trails provided at a typical motorcycle recreation park in Southern California, where off-road riding has become severely restricted by authorities.